Say-young Kim Poetry Collection

English Translation: Euisu Byeon (poet · critic) ▲

시인선 009

별빛의 화법 ⓒ 김세영

초판인쇄 2025. 5. 30.
초판발행 2025. 5. 30.

지은이 김세영
영역 및 펴낸이 변의수
펴낸곳 상징학연구소

출판신고 2022. 1. 22.
신고번호 제 022-000005 호

경기 고양시 일산서구 탄현로 136, 116동 1302호
010-3030-9149
euisu1@hanmail.net
ISBN 979-11-956567-9-0
값 13,000원

잘못된 책은 바꾸어 드립니다.

Narration of Starlight
별빛의 화법

시인의 말

이번 시집에는 최근에 쓴 우주시라고 할 수 있는 장르의 시가 과반이다.

우주시는, "우주에 대한 현대 천체물리학적 사실 인지와 이것을 바탕으로 한 세계 현실의 새로운 인식과 감성으로 쓰여진 시."라고 규정해 본다.

입자에 파동의 속성이 내재 되어 있듯이, 기氣에 리理가 내재 되어 있다고 생각한다. 더 나아가서 물질의 우주세계에는 영성의 우주세계가 내재 되어 있다고 상상해 본다.

이 기파가, 이 에너지 파동의 힘이 우주의 섭리라고 흔히 표현하는 것이라고 생각한다. 이 마음(理)이 우주의 현상에 내재하는 창의적인 원리이며, 우주의 정신 즉 우주의 혼이라고 부를 수 있을 것이다.

미래의 우주시대에서 새로운 시 장르로서, 우주시가 자리매김을 할 수 있기를 기대해 본다. 새로운 약속의 실마리를 암흑 시공간 속에서 모색해본다.

이 시집에 귀한 발문을 써 주신 정과리 문학평론가 연세대학교 명예교수님과 더없이 훌륭한 평론과 추천사를 보내주신 국제적 명성의 시인이자 번역가이며 상징학연구소 편집자문인 마리엘라 코르데로 평론가에게 감사를 드립니다. 아울러, 이 시집의 영어번역 작업과 국내판 및 아마존 동시 출간을 맡아 주신 상징학연구소 변의수 발행인께도 감사를 드립니다.

2024년 한로寒露 ▲

Poet's Word

This anthology is dominated by recent poems in the genre of Cosmic Poetry.

Cosmic Poetry is, "poetry written with a new perception and sensibility of world reality based on modern astrophysical facts perception".

Just as particles inherently possess the properties of waves, I believe that Qi inherently contains the principles of Li. Furthermore, I imagine that the material universe contains the spiritual universe.

I think that the power of this Qi wave, this power of the energy wave, is what is often expressed as the providence of the universe. This mind (Li) is the creative principle inherent in the phenomena of the universe, and can be called the spirit of the universe, that is, the soul of the universe.

I hope that space poetry can establish itself as a new genre of poetry in the future space age. I search for clues of new promise in the darkness of space and time.

I would like to thank Professor Emeritus of Yonsei University, literary critic Gwari Jung, for his valuable afterword to this collection, and Mariela Cordero, an internationally renowned poet, translator, and editorial advisor to the *Symbology Institute*, for her excellent commentary and testimonial. I would also like to thank publisher Euisu Byeon of the *Symbology Institute* for translating this collection of poems into English and simultaneously publishing it in Korea and on Amazon.

At the entrance to fall of 2024 🔺

별빛의 화법
Narration of Starlight

시인의 말
Poet's Words

추천사 Testimonial　　　　　　　　　　　12
마리엘라 코르데로 Mariela Cordero

I
소요유 Roam Freely　　　　　　　　　　20
새로운 약속 The New Covenant　　　　　22
거듭나기 Rebirth　　　　　　　　　　　28
그늘의 빛 Light in Shade　　　　　　　　32
자연스러운 일 Natural Thing　　　　　　36
기화가 되다 Becoming Vapourised　　　　40
우주의 여자 The Woman of Universe　　　44
얽힘 Entanglement　　　　　　　　　　48
울,너머로 Over Fence　　　　　　　　　52
어느 흰나비의 자리 Place of a white butterfly　58
기파의 강 River of Qi Waves　　　　　　62
와디의 기억 Memories on the Wadi　　　　66
오르가슴 Orgasm　　　　　　　　　　　70

바람의 결 Figure of Wind	70
별빛의 화법 Narration of Starlight	76
바오밥 채널 Baobab Channel	80

II

컷 Cut	86
바람의 집 House of Wind	88
가벼움 견습 Lightness Apprenticeship	92
밤의 징검다리 Stepping Stone of Night	94
그림자 무언극 Shadow Pantomime	96
밤낚시 2 Night Fishing 2	100
천등제 Sky Lantern Festival	104
나의 주소지 My Address	108
의자의 회상 Reminiscence of Chair	112
환상통 날개 Phantom Pain Wings	116
춘인 Spring Stamp	120
안단테 칸타빌레 Andante Cantabile	122

젖은 첼로 Wet cello	126
흙 Soil	130
흉터 Scar	132

III
1.0	138
뻘길 Muddy Road	142
겨울 등정 Winter Climbing	144
천산으로 가는 길 Road to Sky Mountain	146
믿음의 뿌리 Roots of Faith	150
풍장 Aerial Sepulture	154
하모니카 주법으로 With harmonica technique	158
죽록원 소요 Bamboo Forest Ramble	160
화석의 꿈 Dream of Fossil	164
나방의 꿈 A Moth's Dream	168
메멘토 모리 Memento Mori	170
잠들기 Falling asleep	174
시계탑 06 Clock Tower 06	178

붉은 연어의 노래 Song of Red Salmon　　　　　182
외치의 꿈 Dream of Ötzi　　　　　　　　　　　186

평론 : 마리엘라 코르데로　　　　　　　　　　190
Commentary :
By Mariela Cordero (Poet · Critic)

나의 우주시론 : 김세영 (시인)　　　　　　　216
My cosmic Poetics : Kim, Say-young(Poet)

발문 : 정과리　　　　　　　　　　　　　　　230
(정명교 : 문학평론가, 연세대 명예교수)
Afterword : Jeong, Gwa-ri
(Jeong, Myeong-gyo: Literary critic,
Professor Emeritus, Yonsei University)

김세영의 우주시론 시집
"별빛의 화법"
절대에 도달하기 위한 여정의 탐구

마리엘라 코르데로
(시인 · 평론가 · 번역가)

시는 상징을 통해 절대에 다가가려는 시도이다". 스페인의 후안 라몬 히메네스(1881~1958)의 이 문구는 유사 이래 수많은 시인들의 탐구 정신을 드러냅니다. 히메네스에 따르면 시는 표현할 수 없는 것을 드러내고 미묘한 상징과 은유를 통해 절대의 세계에 가닿으려 합니다. 그런 히메네스의 작품은 현실과 신비의 세계를 드나들며 진동합니다.

김세영 시인의 시집 『별빛의 화법』 역시 헤아릴 수 없는 광활한 우주에 다가가 절대에 도달하고자 하는 태고의 갈망을 드러낸 작품입니다. 그의 시에서 언급되는 과학 개념들은 천체물리학적 현상에 대한 면밀한 고찰로 드러난 사실과 현실들에 바탕하고 있습니다. 김세영의 시는 양자 물리학과 천체학을 실체적 측면에서 접근합니다.

무한한 우주의 비밀은 위대한 신비의 원천을 이룹니다. 김세영 시인은 과학과 영성을 연결합니다. 그리고 직접 자

Testimonial

Kim, Say-young: Cosmic Poetics Poetry Collection

Narration of Starlight. Seeking to Touch the Absolute.

By Mariela Cordero

Poet-Critic-Translator

《Poetry is an attempt to approach the absolute by means of symbols》. This phrase by the Spanish poet Juan Ramón Jiménez (1881-1958) reveals the quest of countless poets since the beginning of time. Poetry, according to Jiménez, seeks to express the ineffable and touch (even if subtly) the absolute through symbols and metaphors. His poetic work is at the epicenter of a tremor: between reality and mystery.

《Narration of Starlight》 by the poet Kim, Say-young is also on this ancient quest, reflecting this arcane, immemorial thirst for reaching the absolute, approaching the unfathomable vastness of the cosmos. It leans on reality and facts, as the scientific concepts mentioned in his poems reveal a careful investigation into astrophysical phenomena. Kim's poems explore quantum physics and astronomy from a very current perspective.

The infinite cosmos and its secrets represent a great source of mystery. The poet Kim also links science

신의 작품에서 기와 리의 관계를 언급합니다. 리와 기는 개별적 하나로서가 아닌 상호 보완적 관계로 존재합니다. 리는 구조, 질서, 자연법칙을 부여하며, 기는 우주를 드러내고 움직이는 역동적인 힘입니다. 기가 리에 따라 질서를 구현한다면, 리는 질료적 사물과 자연 현상의 전반에 이르기까지 기가 형상적 형태로 조직화되어 나타나게 하는 방법론적 틀입니다.

김세영 작가가 이 시집을 제작하는 데 쏟은 열정과 헌신은 놀랍습니다. 일관된 과학적 이해에 바탕한 방법론을 사용하는 그의 작품은 참으로 감탄스럽습니다. 김세영은 과학적 용어를 단순한 문학적 장식으로 사용하는 것이 아니라, 존재와 우주의 깊이를 탐구하고 표현함으로써 지적으로나 영적으로 공명하는 자세를 취하고 있습니다.

우주의 신비와 심원함을 그려내는 시인은 이 시집을 구성하는 시편들에 우주시라는 이름을 붙였습니다. 별, 행성, 천문 현상의 탐구와 우주적 관조를 통해 철학적, 영적 질문을 모색하는 시인의 시집은 그러한 시적 스타일의 전형을 제시하고 있습니다.

역사의 여러 단계에서 수많은 시인들이 영감적 이유를 찾거나 헤아릴 수 없는 우주의 속성이 불러일으키는 수많은 질문들에 대한 답을 찾기 위해 무한한 밤하늘을 향해 시선을 들어 올렸습니다. 우주적 시선 또는 비전을 가진 시인들은 역사적 시대의 관점에서 우주에 자신만의 용어와 언어로 이름을 붙였으며, 우주에 대한 인간 지식의 진화를 점진적으로 투영해나갔습니다. 김세영 시인의 작품은 이러한 맥락의 다각적인 접근 방식이 돋보입니다.

그의 시에는 양자 물리학과 새로운 이론, 우주의 비밀에 대한 새로운 개념과 깊은 연구가 드러나 있습니다. 김세영

with spirituality. In the introduction the poet himself makes to his work, he references the relationship between Qi and Li. Li and Qi complement each other and cannot exist without one another. Li provides the structure, order, and natural laws, while Qi is the dynamic force that animates and moves the universe. Qi needs Li to manifest in an orderly way. Li is the framework that guides how Qi is organized and manifests in tangible forms, from physical objects to natural phenomena.

The passion and dedication with which Kim, Say-young has crafted this anthology is remarkable. He has relied on a method based on consistent scientific understanding, and this is worthy of admiration. Kim is not content with using scientific terms as mere literary adornments; instead, he uses these concepts to delve into and express the depths of existence and the cosmos in a way that resonates both intellectually and spiritually.

The poet Kim refers to the poetry that makes up this anthology as cosmic poetry. This poetry seeks to express the mysteries and grandeur of the universe through language. This type of poetry explores the infinitude of space, the stars, the planets, and astronomical phenomena, as well as the philosophical and spiritual questions that arise when contemplating the universe. With this compilation of poems, the poet aspires to become a reference in this poetic style.

At different stages of history, numerous poets have lifted their gaze to the sky, to the infinite or nocturnal azure in search of reasons for inspiration or in search of answers to the thousands of questions that arise before the unfathomable nature of the universe. These poets, with their cosmic gaze or vision, have named the universe from the perspective of their historical time, in their own terms and words, gradually reflecting the evolution of

시인의 이 독특한 관점은 단순히 희열과 열정을 드러내려는 것이 아니라, 탄탄한 지식의 뒷받침과 정교한 방식으로 그 분출을 전달하는 방법을 보여주고 있습니다.『별빛의 화법』에서 과학과 시적 예술의 결합은 김세영 시인이 첨단의 과학 개념과 깊은 서정적 표현의 통합으로 새로운 표현 형식의 선구자가 되게 합니다.

김세영 시인의 작품은 그러한 목적을 달성하고 초월하는 기준이 된다고 결론을 내릴 수 있습니다. 우주적 렌즈를 통해 보편적 주제를 다루고 통합하는 그의 능력은 미래의 시인들에게 높은 기준을 제시해 놓고 있습니다. 그의 시 형식은 분명 다른 이들로 하여금 명백해 보이는 세계 너머의 과학적 지식과 예술적 창의성 사이의 연관성을 탐구하도록 영감을 줄 것입니다.

라몬 히메네스는 항상 언어를 통해 시인이 절대의 세계에 도달하려 한다고 하였습니다만, 김세영 시인이『별빛의 화법』에서 절대적인 것, 닿을 수 없는 것에 다가가고자 하는 것이 바로 그것입니다. 그는 시를 통해 인간 지식의 한계를 탐구하고 심층 우주를 파고들어 존재에 관한 더욱 풍부하고 향상된 시각을 제공합니다.

저는 김세영 시인의『별빛의 화법』이 특정 장르로서의 우주 시의 토대를 마련하고자 하는 문학과 시의 역사에서 중요한 이정표라고 굳게 믿습니다. 아울러, 참신성과 독창성을 고대하는 시문학의 독자 누구나 즐겨 읽을 수 있으며 또한, 이러한 시의 스타일에서 피할 수 없는 전범으로 김세영 시인의 작품은 자리매김하리라고 단언합니다. ◣

human knowledge about the cosmos. Kim, Say-young's work stands out in this context for its versatile approach.

In his poetry, an exhaustive investigation into quantum physics, new theories, and emerging concepts about the secrets of the universe is revealed. This peculiar perspective is not just a display of euphoria and enthusiasm, but the poet has known how to channel this effusion in a sophisticated manner, backing it up with solid knowledge. The combination of science and poetic art in ≪Narration of Starlight≫ makes Kim a precursor of new forms of expression, by integrating advanced scientific concepts with a deep lyrical expression.

I can conclude that Kim, Say-young's work achieves its purpose and becomes a transcendental reference. His ability to address and merge universal themes through a cosmic lens sets a high standard for future poets. His style will surely inspire others to look beyond the obvious and explore the connections between scientific knowledge and artistic creativity.

As I mentioned, Juan Ramón Jiménez considers that the poet always tries to reach the absolute through words. That is precisely what Kim does in ≪Narration of Starlight≫; he seeks to reach and touch the absolute and the ineffable. Through his poetry, Kim explores the limits of human knowledge and delves into the depths of the universe, offering the reader an enhanced and enriched vision of existence.

I firmly believe that the poetry anthology ≪Narration of Starlight≫ by the poet Kim, Say-young represents a significant milestone in the history of literature and poetry as it intends to lay the foundations of cosmic poetry as a particular genre. I can assert that Kim's work positions itself as an unavoidable reference in this style of poetry and its reading will be enjoyed by all those seekers of the novel and original in the literary field. ▲

I

소요유 逍遙遊

알을 깨고 나온 누에의 몸털처럼
갓 우화한 어린 날개의 깃털처럼

대숲을 빠져나온 바람처럼 자유롭게
한바탕 울음을 쏟은 구름처럼 홀가분하게

별들의 소리가 선명해지는
자정의 몽유처럼
꿈꾸며 노닐자

육신의 틀을 벗은 혼령처럼
입자의 틀을 벗은 파동처럼
시공의 틀을 벗은 양자처럼

달을 품은 백학의 날개처럼
춤추며 노닐자.

Roam Freely

Like silkworm's silk breaking free
Like young wing's feather unfurled

Like wind escaping bamboo forest, free
Like cloud bursting into tears, carefree

Stars sound's growing clearer
Like dream of midnight
Let me play, dreaming

Like spirit shedding body frame
Like waves escaping particles pattern
Like quanta transcending space—time form

Like white crane wings cradling the moon
Let me roam freely, dancing

새로운 약속 新約

여명의 돔 위에 앉아있는
저 이글거리는 잔

겹겹이 쌓인 암흑물질1)을
홍염으로 태우고
거대한 빛을 뿜어올린다

창세를 열었던 입술,
오래된 약속의 지문이 묻어있는
눈부신 황금 성배聖杯!

저 잔 속에 무엇이 있을까?

백억 년의 암흑에너지 속에서
숙성한 신의 술일까?

저 금단의 술을 훔쳐 마시고
우주알의 껍질을 깨트리고 부화시키는
우주새의 혼이 불꽃으로 솟아 오른다

시공간에 흩뿌려진 별들, 혼불의 파동
팽창하는 별자리들, 이합집산의 문양들

The New Covenant

Sitting atop the dome of dawn
That blazing cup
Layer upon layer of dark matter[1]
Burning by prominence
Emitting mighty light

Lip opened creation,
With fingerprint of ancient promise
The brilliant golden Holy Grail!

What's in that cup?

Within dark energy for ten billion years
Might it be the divine wine aged?

Stealing, drinking that forbidden wine
Cracking, hatching cosmic egg shell
A soul of cosmic bird, soaring in flame

Stars scattered across space−time, wave of soul fire
 Expanding constellations, patterns merging and scattering

출렁이는 은하의 파도,
쓰나미파²⁾로 몰려오는
우주의 종소리와 박동이
정수리 천문泉門의 수상돌기를 흔든다

은하의 원류를 찾아서
헬리오포즈³⁾를 벗어나는 보이저처럼
태양계를 벗어나는 혼령들의 환희

성간을 건너가는 혜성처럼
입자의 틀을 빠져나온 파동처럼
주파수 공명을 찾아서 합류하며
장대한 기파의 강이 흐른다

궁수자리 A별⁴⁾의 중심부를 뚫고
물질 우주의 웜홀⁵⁾을 지나
화이트홀⁶⁾ 너머로
오로라처럼 솟구쳐 나가서
영성 우주로 건너갈 거야

우주새의 전언傳言처럼
새로운 약속의 예언대로
거대한 기파의 공명, 끝없는 성간 울림
영성의 법열로 거듭날 수 있을 거야.

1) 우주에 존재하는 물질의 대부분은 26.8%를 차지하는 암흑물질이다. 보통의 물질은 4.9% 정도이고, 나머

The waves of galaxy undulating,
Advancing tsunami waves[2]
Cosmic bell sound and pulses
Shaking dendrites of crown fontanelle

Seeking galaxy origin
Like Voyager leaving heliopause[3]
Spirits ecstasy leaving solar system

Like comet crossing interstellar
Like waves escaping particle frame
Finding, joining frequencies resonance
The mighty Qi[4] waves river flowing

Piercing through Sgr A[5] heart
Passing through material universe wormhole[6]
Beyond white hole[7]
Soaring forward like aurora
Will going to cross into spiritual universe

Like cosmic bird message
As prophesied in new covenant
Great Qi waves' resonance, endless interstellar echos
Will be reborn in spiritual Dharma bliss.

1) Most of the matter in the universe is dark matter, which accounts for 26.8%. Ordinary matter makes up about 4.9 per cent, and the remaining 68.3 per cent is

지 68.3%는 아직 정체를 모르는 '암흑 에너지'이다.
2) 성간(interstellar)에서 우주의 이온화 가스물질인 플라즈마가 종이 울리듯 진동하며 생기는 우주파.
3) 성간 공간을 통해 쏟아져 들어오는 강력한 우주선과 태양풍이 충돌하는 이 거품 영역의 가장자리에 있는 뜨겁고 두꺼운 플라스마 장벽.
4) 궁수자리 A(에이 스타)는 우리 은하의 중심에 위치한 태양의 400만 배의 질량을 가진 초대형 블랙홀.
5) 블랙홀과 화이트홀을 연결하는 우주 시공간의 구멍. 웜홀을 지나 성간 여행이나 은하 간 여행을 할 때, 짧은 시간에 우주의 한쪽에서 다른 쪽으로 도달할 수 있다.
6) 블랙홀과 대척 관계. 우주 에너지를 방출하는, 이론적 가상의 특이점.

'dark energy', whose identity is still unknown.
2) A cosmic wave caused by the interstellar oscillation of ionised gaseous matter, plasma, in the universe, like a bell ringing.
3) A hot, thick plasma barrier at the edge of this bubble region, where powerful cosmic rays and solar winds pouring through interstellar space collide.
4) The fundamental element of matter. (Translator's note)
5) Sagittarius A (A Star) is a supermassive black hole with a mass four million times that of the Sun located at the centre of our galaxy.
6) A hole in space-time that connects a black hole to a white hole. When travelling interstellar or intergalactic through a wormhole, one can get from one side of the universe to the other in a short time.
7) The opposite of a black hole. A theoretical, hypothetical singularity that emits cosmic energy.

거듭나기

수상돌기[1]에 붙어사는 환생의 뿌리혹들,
히드라[2]처럼 다중의 생을 품고 살아
머리통을 옥죄는 데자뷰의 덩굴들

때때로 군발성 두통으로
불면의 덫에 갇힌다

그럴 때마다 별자리 속으로 가지 치는
굿바위 산의 당산나무 밑에 선다

바오밥 나무가 된 듯
머리카락이 신경다발처럼 곤추선다

북극성에서 방출한 혼령의 빛이
뇌회(腦回)[3]의 레지스트리[4]에 기생하는
악령을 제거하고 최적화시킨다

아득한 시공간 너머로부터
양자도약(量子跳躍)[5]으로 다가온
새로운 생의 기파 마디들을
방전된 우주선을 공중 충전하듯
정수리 천문으로 주입시킨다

가끔씩,

Rebirth

Reincarnate nodules clinging to dendrites,[1)]
Living with multiple lives like hydra[2)]
Imprisoning head, vines of déjà vu

Sometimes with cluster headaches
Trapping in sleeplessness trap

Stretching branches into constellations, whenever happens
Standing beneath a Gudbawi-mountain dangsan-tree[3)]

As if a baobab tree
Hair stands on end like a bundle of nerves

Spirit light emitted from North Star
Removing and optimising evil spirit
Parasitising in a gyrus'[4)] registry[5)]

Beyond faraway space-time
Arrived through quantum jump[6)]
Qi wave nodes of new life
Like recharging a discharged spaceship in midair
Injecting into a crown fontanelle

새로운 아침에 일어나
낯선 듯한 거울 속의 모습을 보면서
타인 같은 나를 탈감작[6]시킨다

아침 신문처럼 새로운
또 하루의 이야기를 써보자고

1) 신경전달 물질을 받아들이는 신경세포 머리 부분의 돌기.
2) 그리스신화에 나오는 머리가 여러 개인 괴물 뱀.
3) 대뇌의 표면에서 밭의 이랑이나 둑처럼 솟은 부분.
4) 윈도우 시스템에서 사용하는 시스템 구성 정보를 저장한 데이터베이스.
5) 양자역학적으로 시공간을 초월한, 영성 파동의 비국소적 운동성.
6) 어떤 항원에 대하여 과민 상태에 있는 개체의 과민성을 없애는 처치.

Occasionally,

Waking up on new morning
Looking at unfamiliar face in mirror
Desensitizing[7] me like others

New like morning newspaper
Vowing to write story of day again

> 1) A projection on the head of a nerve cell that receives neurotransmitters.
> 2) hydra: A multi-headed monster snake from Greek mythology.
> 3) A name given to a tree on a mountain that is believed to be inhabited by a spirit and for which ancestral rites are held, related to Korean indigenous beliefs. (Translator's note)
> 4) The part of the cerebrum that rises from the surface of the brain like a gyrus or bank in a field.
> 5) A database that stores system configuration information used by Windows systems.
> 6) The non-local motion of a spiritual wave, quantum mechanically transcending space and time.
> 7) A treatment that removes the hypersensitivity of an individual to an antigen.

그늘의 빛

여름산의 중심에 서 있는
상수리나무 그늘의 기공氣孔 속에
뿌리혹처럼 빛들이 숨어있다

열기의 정점, 정오의 상수리는
수천의 매미들이 한꺼번에 울 때
커다란 솜사탕으로 부푼 울음덩어리가 된다

그 울음소리에 잎사귀 뒷면의
푸른 빛 알갱이들이 아우라로 피어올라
집광판 이마를 식혀준다

자정, 그늘의 심저에서 발원한
검은 태풍의 몰이에
수만의 청어 떼가 질주할 때

불안에 떠는 눈알들이 서로 부딪혀
번뜩이는 빛 회오리 되어
고양이 눈 성운 속으로 빨려 들어간다

어깨선 높은 산 그리매 속,
등이 긴 사람의 갈비뼈 그림자,
묵언의 새장, 그 촘촘한 행간 사이로, 설핏

Light in Shade

Standing in centre of summer mountain
In stomas of oak shade
Hiding of light like nodule

Peak of heat, Noonday tree
While thousands cicadas chirping at once
Becoming large cotton-candy puffing-up cry

With Cry, blue light particles on leaves' back
Blooming into Aura
Cooling light-collector forehead

At midnight, from depths of shadow
Due to Black storm
Sprinting of tens thousands herrings

Crashing anxious eyeballs
Becoming light whirlwinds
Sucking into Cat-eye nebula

In shoulder-high mountain shade,
Shadow of long-backed man rib,
Silent cage, through its tight rows, momently

전류처럼 박동하는 새벽별 빛이 보인다

발꿈치 뼈 골수 속 빛의 싹들이,
기공 속 그늘의 빛들이,
가장 낮은 곳에서 가장 높은 곳으로
뇌량腦梁 위 시냅스[1]로 올라간
정수리 천문의 기파들이,

북극성 별자리 중력의 당김으로
귀천하는 오로라처럼
궁륭을 가르며 솟구쳐 오른다.

    1) 하나의 신경 세포와 신경 섬유를 신경 단위라고 하는데, 이 신경 단위 상호 간의 접합부.

Seeing dawn starlight pulsing like current

Buds of light in marrow of heel bone,
Lights of shade in stomas,
From the lowest to the highest
Rising to synapses[1] above corpus callosum
Qi waves of parietal fontanelle,

With gravitational pull of Polaris
Like aurora going back to heaven
Soaring through vault.

> 1) The connection site of a nerve unit consisting of one nerve cell and a nerve fibre.

자연스러운 일

개망초 꽃잎이 발에 밟혀도
매미가 솔방울처럼 발길에 차여도
산책길에서는 자연스러운 일이다

깨어있는 많은 날
노심초사 심지를 다 태워 버리고
안식의 집에 들어가는 것도
자연스러운 퇴장이다

세상에 갇혀 살았으니, 이제는
벌거숭이 천문의 시냅스를
당산나무 가지처럼
언덕에 세우면 된다

굽은 손가락 사이로
마지막 남은 기파가 빠져나갈 때까지

손바닥 속, 이승의 기억을
벽조목 염주처럼 여물어지도록
매만지고 다듬는 것이
나의 마지막, 자연스러운 일이다.

붕어빵 한 봉지의 뼛가루로

Natural Thing

While fleabane petals are tramped underfoot
Cicada kicked by foot like pinecone
Natural, walking the path

Many waking days
Burning all worried wicks
Also entering house of rest
Is natural exit

Having lived trapped in world. now
Naked fontanel synapse
Like branches of dangsan-tree[1)]
Let's set on hill

Between bent fingers
Until last remaining Qi wave has escaped

In palm, memory of this life
Until hardens like jujube prayer beads
Polishing and refining
My last, natural act.

Like bone powder of a fish-shaped bread bag

산의 풀숲에 뿌려지는 것도
자연스러운 마무리이다

보이저호가 헬리오포즈[1]를 벗어나듯
우주여행을 떠나는 것은
자연스러운 버킷리스트이다

상여 노래를 애달피 부르지 마라
흑인 영가라도 흥겹게 부를 일이다
흰나비처럼 날개 펄럭이며
버선코 세우고 승무를 출 일이다.

    1) 성간 공간을 통해 쏟아져 들어오는 강력한 우주선과 태양풍이 충돌하는 이 거품 영역의 가장자리에 있는 뜨겁고 두꺼운 플라스마 장벽.

Also scattering in mountain grass
Is natural ending

Like Voyager leaving heliopause[2]
Space travelling
Is a natural bucket list

Don't sing death song with sorrow
Sing even a black spiritual with joy
Fluttering wings like white butterfly,
Lift up socks toe, dance Buddhist dancing

> 1) A name given to a tree that is believed to be inhabited by a spirit and for which ancestral rites are held, related to Korean indigenous beliefs. (Translator's note)
> 2) A hot, thick plasma barrier at the edge of this bubble region, where powerful cosmic rays and solar winds pouring through interstellar space collide.

기화氣化가 되다

팔 할이, 공기로 되어 있다

칠십 년 이상 공기를 마시고 살아온 탓에
육신이 풍선처럼 부풀어

바람 든 무처럼
뼈에 구멍이 숭숭 뚫리고 있다
마른 황태처럼
피부 껍질이 투명해지고
근육이 육포처럼 얇아진다

피복이 벗겨진 노후 된 전선처럼
신경초神經鞘가 벗겨진 감각신경이
외부 자극에 민감해진다
가벼운 터치나 스킨십에도
찌릿찌릿, 정전기 스파크가 생긴다

감성지수가 높아져서
칠순이 지난 나이에도 철 지난 사춘기이다
세상 욕심을 내려놓으니 영육이 가벼워진다
만화방창[1] 춘몽과 월하독작[2] 몽상에 취해 산다
취중의 넋두리로 음유시인 행세하며 산다

Becoming Vapourised

Because more than seventy years of breathing air

Body is inflated like balloon
Eighty per cent, is made of air

Like wind-soaked radish
Bones are pierced with holes
Like skinny walleye pollack
Skin is transparent
Muscles thin as jerky

Like old wires stripped of sheath
Sensory nerves stripped of neurilemmas
Become sensitive to external stimulus
Even with light touches or skinships
Tingling, static sparks appearing

Because emotional index is high
Even though over seventy, still immature puberty
Giving up worldly desires, body and soul become lighter.
Living intoxicated with manwhoabangchang[1] spring dream and weolhadokjac[2] fancies
Living as a minstrel in drunken mutters

육신이, 믹서기로 간 듯 미세입자가 되고 있다
살점이 드라이아이스(dry ice)처럼
기체로 서서히 승화되고 있다
정신이, 오르가슴의 신열에 기파로 증류되고 있다

틀에서 벗어난 기파가 양자도약[3]으로
천문泉門의 수상돌기가 가리키는 대로
어느 때 어디에나 직방 닿을 수 있다

영성靈性 자유, 날마다
기화가 되어가고 있다.

       1) 따뜻한 봄이 되어 온갖 생물이 나서 자람.
       2) 달 아래 홀로 술을 마시며, 이백李白의 시.
       3) 양자역학적으로 시공간을 초월한, 영성 파동의 비국소적 운동성.

Body, becoming fine particles, as if grinded in blender
Like dry ice, flesh
Is slowly sublimating into gas
Mind is distilling into Qi waves in heat of orgasm

Unconventional Qi waves with quantum jump[3]
As dendrites of fontanelle point out
Can reach anywhere, anytime, instantly

Spirituality freedom, day by day
becoming vapourised

> 1) In the warm spring, all kinds of living things come out and grow. (Translator's note)
> 2) Drinking alone under the moon, a poem by Lee Baek. (Translator's note)
> 3) The non−local mobility of spiritual waves, transcending space and time in quantum mechanics.

우주의 여자

은하의 고독한 불씨로 던져져
팽창하는 자유의 횃불

암흑에너지를 품고 사는
중년의 독신녀

불꽃의 절반을 태우며
갱년기에 접어든 여왕

적색 거성, 거대한 적혈구의 용광로
심장이 불꽃을 뿜는다

그녀를 연모하는 뭇 행성들
홍염紅焰의 치맛자락에 휩싸인다

별똥별들,
한여름 밤의 불나방처럼
열락의 분신을 한다

늪처럼 깊은 자궁의 내막 속
오랜 욕망에 지친 흰 뼈를 묻으려는
백색 왜성들의 수억 마리의 꿈들,

모천처럼 찾아가는 블랙홀이

The Woman of Universe

Casting as lone embers of galaxy
Expanding torch of freedom

Living with dark energy
Middle−aged bachelorette

Burning half flame
The Queen in menopause

Red giant star, huge furnace of red cells
Heart breathes flame

Many planets adoring her
Are engulfed by skirt of prominence

Shooting stars,
Like fire moths on midsummer night
Burning themselves in delight

In swampy depths of endometrium
To bury white bones, weary from long desires
Hundreds million dreams of white dwarfs,

Black hole seeking like mother stream

그녀의 단전 속에 있음이다

때로는 여왕벌처럼 외롭고 슬플 때
울먹임의 파도가 은하의 유역에 범람한다
쓰나미에 떠내려간 유성들이
궤도를 잃은 우주의 유랑자가 된다

훗날, 마지막 몸 보시 다비
초신성超新星의 광채로
우주의 등대가 되려는 그녀!

떠도는 혼의 유성들을 초혼가로 부른다
우주의 어머니, 용광로 가슴으로
얼음 운석이 된 심장들을 품어준다

새로운 별의 마그마로 채워주려는 것이다.

Because it is within her abdomen

Sometimes, when lonely and sad like Queen bee
Waves of weeping flood galactic basin
Meteors washed out in tsunamis
Become cosmic wanderers lost in orbit

Later, final almsgiving cremation
With brilliance of Supernova
She wanting to become beacon of universe!

Singing meteors of wandering souls
Mother of Universe, with furnace bosom
Embracing hearts become icy meteorites

To fill them with magma of new stars.

얽힘[1]

내가 보는
내가 느끼는
내가 상상하는
상들이 중첩[2]되어 있다

경극京劇의 변신처럼
상들이 썼다 벗었다
시시각각 변한다

밤하늘,
은하의 나선 고리에 얽혀
상들이 도미노처럼
일어나고 쓰러진다

별자리들,
멀리 떨어져 있어도
그리움의 고리에 꿰여
언제나 함께 깜박이며
설레인다

암흑에너지 기층 너머에서
번져와서 흩날리는
끝없는 기파의 줄기들

Entanglement[1]

My seeing
My feeling
My imagining
Images are superposed[2]

Like transformation of Beijing opera
Statues put on, take off
Change every moment

Night sky,
Entangled in spiral ring of galaxy
Statues, like domino
Rising, falling

Constellations,
Even though far apart
Threaded in ring of longing
Always blinking together
Fluttering

From beyond Qi layers of dark energy
Spreading, scattering
Endless stalks of Qi wave

수없는 혼령의 꽃잎들

쉼 없이 이어오는
파동의 리듬
상의 이합집산

주파수의 공명을 찾아서
오묘한 화음을 따라서
기파의 선율이 울려 퍼진다

언제 어디서나 함께
율려律呂[3]로 출렁인다.

1) 한 번 짝을 이룬 두 입자들은 아무리 서로 멀리 떨어져 있다 하더라도, 어느 한 쪽이 변동하면 그에 따라 '즉각' 다른 한 쪽이 반응을 보이는 불가사의한 양자역학의 특성
2) 양자중첩은 여러 상태가 확률적으로 하나의 양자에 동시에 존재하며, 측정하기 전까지는 양자 상태를 정확히 알 수 없는 상태.
3) 율려는 우주의 무궁한 조화가 일어나는 바탕자리 즉 본성이며, 우주만물이 태어나는 생명의 근원이며, 창조정신의 근원이다.

Countless petals of spirit

Continuing without rest
Rhythms of wave
Meeting and parting of images

Searching for resonance in frequencies
Following subtle chord
Qi wave melodies resound

Anytime, anywhere, together
With Yullyeo[3] fluctuating

> 1) A mysterious property of quantum mechanics in which two particles, once paired, respond 'instantaneously' to any change in one, no matter how far apart they are.
> 2) A state in which multiple states probabilistically exist simultaneously in a single quantum, and the exact state of the quantum is unknown until it is measured.
> 3) The source of life and the creative spirit from which all things in the universe are born, the ground from which the infinite harmony of the universe arises.

울(울타리), 너머로

사지 근육이 약해지고
직립 균형이 약해지고
심장 박동이 약해지고
신경 전달이 약해지고

불안한 날들이 쌓이고
불면의 밤들이 쌓이고
무념의 시간이 쌓이고
무상의 공간이 쌓이고

언제부터인가 야윈 가슴통을
탱자나무 울이 둘러싸고 있다

이 울이
최후의 전신갑주全身甲冑가 되고
세상으로부터 도피처가 될 수 있을까?

이 울이
위리안치圍籬安置의 거처가 되고
종신형의 독방이 되는 것인가?

덫 속의 짐승처럼 바동거리다
나갈 의지도 잃어가고

Over Fence

Limb muscles become weak
Upright balance weakens
Heartbeats weak
Nerve transmission weakens

Uneasy days pile up
Sleepless nights pile up
Mindless hours pile up
Emptying space piles up

Since when lean chest
Tangza tree[1] fence surrounds

This fence
Becomes last jeonsinkabju[2]
Can be refuge from the world?

This fence
Becomes abode of Wirianchi[3]
Solitary for life sentence?

Writhing like animal in trap
Losing will to escape

나갈 길도 잊어가고 있다

때로는
고용량 알프라졸람[1]의 안락함 속에 빠져보기도,
망각의 압착기 속에 머리를 넣어보기도 한다

고달팠던 기억 저장, 가득
가슴 아픈 기억 저장, 가득
후회스런 기억 저장, 가득
즐거웠던 기억 저장, 조금
마른 해마의 주머니 속에 담겨 있다

육신의 인연에 얽매이지 말자
불안과 두려움의 단어는 잊자
손바닥에 마지막까지 쓸 수 있는 글자, 잊지 말자
용서해 주세요
감사합니다

들숨과 날숨을 멈춘 후
탱자나무 줄기로 염을 하면
마른 육포의 미라
무덤이 되겠지.

자유혼아, 기화되어
중력의 울(울타리)을 헤치고 나와
공명의 기파를 쫓아가자

우주의 새로운 거처,

Forgetting way out

Sometimes
Try to slip into comfort of high−dose alprazolam[4],
To put head in press of oblivion

Painful memories stored, full
Heartbreaking memories, full.
Regretful memories, full
Pleasant memories, a little
Is in pocket of dried−up seahorse

Let's not be bound by fleshly fetters
Let's forget words of anxiety and fear
Let's not forget the last words writable on palm
Please forgive me
Thank you

After stopping inhalation and exhalation
Yeom[5] with trunks of a tangja tree
Mummy of dried jerky
Become grave.

Free spirit, vapourised
Come out through fence of gravity
Let's chase Qi waves of resonance

New residence in universe,

영성 세계로 가자.

1) 알프라졸람은 벤조디아제핀 계열에 속하는 약물로 뇌에서 신경흥분을 억제하여 불안, 공황장애 등의 치료에 사용된다.

To world of spirituality.

1) tangja tree: A tree about three metres tall, with small leaves with serrated teeth. It has ball-shaped yellow fruits. (Translator's note)
2) Armour and helmet covering the whole body. (Translator's note)
3) Wianrichi: a hedge of thorns around a house, and exiled sinners were kept in it. (Translator's note)
4) Alprazolam is a drug belonging to the benzodiazepine family that inhibits nerve excitement in the brain and is used to treat anxiety, panic disorder, etc.
5) The act of dressing a corpse in new clothes and wrapping it in cloth or blankets. (Translator's note)

어느 흰나비의 자리

1초도 멈출 수 없는 초침바늘처럼
팔랑이는 날갯짓,
일렁이는 공명의 바람,
확성기처럼 숲의 그늘을 흔든다

온종일 제 몸 틀을 찾아
꽃들을 기웃거리는 방황의 끝

멈추어 선 자리, 언제이든가
낯설게 보이지 않는 저 꽃 자리!

그늘 속 흰빛의 편린,
기억 저편의 체취!

어두워지기 전, 허둥지둥
꽃잎에 날개의 문양을 맞추어 본다

오랜 섭생의 침낭인양
그의 혼령이 스며든다

볼록렌즈의 초점처럼 한 점에 모여지는
그 향기의 깊숙한 속
네 꿈과 생의 발원 점이었지

Place of a white butterfly

Like a second hand unstoppable even for a second.
Fluttering wings,
Rippling wind of resonance,
Shaking shade of forest like loudspeaker

All day long searching for own body shape
End of wanderings among flowers

Place where stopped, when
That flower spot not looking unfamiliar!

A piece of white light in shade,
Body odour beyond memory!

Before gets dark, hurriedly
Trying to match pattern of wings to petal

As if sleeping bag of long regimen
His spirit seeping in

Converging on one point, like focus of convex lens
Deep within that fragrance
The origin of your dreams and life

두툼한 환생의 갈피 속
한 가닥의 기파

오랜 탐색의 끝에 재회한
거듭나는 생의 몸틀
데자뷰의 요람일 거야

첫 기억의 특이점特異點[1]인가?

1) 빅뱅 우주의 시작점.

In thick veil of rebirth
One strand Qi wave

Reunited after long search
Reborn body figure of life
Maybe cradle of déjà vu

The singularity of first memories[1] Is it?

1) The beginning of the Big Bang Universe.

기파氣波의 강

별들의 검은 무덤 너머
화이트홀[1]에서 발원한
영성靈性의 강이 흐른다

수면 위로 눈부시게 춤추는 기파들
수면 아래로 도도하게 흐르는 기파들
우주를 건너가는 혼의 은하이다

재탄생한 기파덩이들이
다도해의 섬처럼 떠다니는
빛의 강에는 나선의 파동들이
오로라로 피어오른다

해초처럼 일렁이는 기파의 무리들이
수십 억 년 시공 속에서 운집한
거대한 기류의 파고波高를 이룬다

주파수 공명에 따라 이합집산하듯
인연의 매듭이 다시 얽히고 풀리듯
혼령의 백학들이 군무를 춘다

새롭게 거듭난 혼별들이
율려의 음표를 되짚으며

River of Qi Waves

Beyond black graves of stars
From white hole[1)]
River of spirituality flows

Qi waves dazzlingly dancing on water surface
Qi waves flowing lazily beneath surface
Is galaxy of souls crossing universe

Reborn Qi wave masses
Floating like islands in the Dadohae[2)]
Spiral waves in river of light
Bloom as aurora

Swarms of Qi wave rippling like seaweed
Gathered in billions years' time−space
Forming huge waves of Qi currents

As Converging and dispersing along frequency resonance
As knots of fate tangle and untangle again
White cranes of spirits dance round

Newly reborn spirit stars
As retracing notes of yeollyeo[3)]

우주의 영성 바다로 흘러간다

지난 생의 강들을 건너오며
부르던 상여의 가락을
환청으로 되새기며 유영한다

부드러운 물성物性과 아릿한 정감,
눈부신 색광色光의 신기루...
아득한 기억들을 잊지 못하여
끝없는 양자도약[2]의 환생을 꿈꾼다.

1) 블랙홀과 대척관계에 있으며. 우주의 에너지 방출을 하는, 이론적 가상의 특이점.
2) 영성 파동의, 양자역학적으로 시공간을 초월한 비국소적 운동성.

Flowing into cosmic spiritual ocean

Crossing rivers of past life
Tune of death song
Swimming while reminiscing with hallucinations

Soft materiality and piquant emotion,
Mirage of dazzling colour light...
Can't forget faraway memories
Dreaming reincarnation through endless quantum jumps[4].

> 1) white hole: Opposite of black hole. A theoretical hypothetical singularity that emits the energy of the universe.
> 2) A maritime national park that spans from Dolsan Island to Hongdo Island in Yeosu, Jeollanam-do, South Korea. (Translator's note)
> 3) The source of life and the creative spirit from which all things in the universe are born, the ground from which the infinite harmony of the universe arises. (Translator's note)
> 4) Spiritual wave, quantum mechanical, non-local motion beyond space and time.

와디(Wadi)의 기억

푸른 기억들이 넘쳐흐르던 강이었지
은하수의 별들이 강물로 녹아들었지

이제는 낯설게도 보이는
모래산 골짜기 사이로
마른 핏줄 덩굴이 기어가고 있다

모천의 체취를 못 잊어서
강을 거슬러 왔다가 죽은
해마海馬들의 체액과
마른 이끼가 바닥을 덮고 있다

이끼의 흔적을 맡으며
와디(Wadi)를 걸어가 본다
모래톱 위의 깨어진 기억들
사금파리처럼 가슴을 찌른다

은하로 흘러가 버린
그녀가 주고간 모래 시간들
일 초당 기억 한 알씩
목줄로 흘러내렸다

횡격막 위에서 쌓이고 쌓여

Memories on the Wadi

Was river overflowing with blue memories.
Milky Way's stars melted into the river

Now, seeming also unfamiliar
Through valleys of sandy mountain
Dried blood vessel vines crawling

Can't forget smell of mother
Died after travelling up river
Seahorses fluids and
Dried moss is covering ground

As smelling trail of moss
Walking through the wadi
Broken memories on sandbank
Stinging my chest like saguempari[1]

Flowed away to galaxy
Sandy time she left behind
One grain of memory each second
Flowing down through the gullet

Piled up and piled up on diaphragm

허파꽈리 탑이 되었다
수억의 기억들이 들어와 사는
흰개미 탑이다

그녀 가슴팍의 마른 실핏줄이
와디의 모래탑을 기어오르며
개미핥기처럼 기억을 더듬는다

보름달 뜨면 폐포 속으로
만조로 가득 차오르는
그녀의 환생 기파
들숨과 날숨으로 가슴 부푼다

귀에 익은 강물 소리 속으로
폐엽에 박힌 파편들을 침례浸禮하며
환생하는 해마처럼
기억 속의 태아처럼 유영해 간다.

Became tower of alveolas
With hundreds millions of memories
Termite mound

Dry capillary of her chest
Climbing sand towers of wadi
Groping for memories like anteaters

When full moon rises, into alveolus
Filling up like high tide
Her reincarnation Qi wave
Chest swelling up with inhalation and exhalation

Into familiar river sound
Baptising fragments embedded in lung lobes
Like reviving seahorse
Swimming like fetus in memory.

    1) Small pieces of broken pottery. (Translator's note)

오르가슴

화심花心의 수렁 속을 탐지하는
환각의 돌기들이여!

육신의 즙을 증발시키는
감성의 분무기여!

감각의 단애를 건너가는
날개의 촉수들이여!

신기루로 펼쳐지는
몽환의 프리즘인가?

오로라 위로 솟구치는
몽상의 비상인가?

화이트홀[1] 너머로 빠져나가는
기파의 환생인가?

은하의 골짜기를 비추는
기파氣波의 빛이여!
영성靈性의 법열이여!

1) white hole: 블랙홀과 대척관계에 있으며, 우주의 에너지를 방출하는, 이론적 가상의 특이점.

Orgasm

Protrusions of psychedelia!
Detecting mire of flower's heart

Atomiser of sensibility!
Evaporating juice of flesh

Tentacles of wings!
Crossing chasm of sensation

Are prisms of dream?
Unfolding into mirage

Flight of dream?
Soaring above aurora

Reincarnation of Qi wave?
Escaping beyond white hole[1]

Light of Qi wave!
Illuminating galactic valley
Rapture of Spirituality!

> 1) The opposite of a black hole. A theoretical hypothetical singularity that emits the energy of the universe.

바람의 결

바람의 손끝이
벼랑을 스칠 때마다
현을 튕기는 소리 들린다

손끝으로 더듬어보면
엘피판의 홈 같은
수많은 문양의 결이 촉지된다

지상을 떠난 혼을 부르며
수천수만 번 뜯는 바람의 탄주
손끝에 핏자국을 남기듯
바위에 홈을 판 것인가?

목숨들의 숨소리가 고이면
골짜기와 반석, 어디든
기파의 홈이 파이겠지

시간의 협곡 속 깊숙이
해초의 암반 화석에서,
단층 속 암모나이트 껍질에서

가슴 후비듯 절절하면
달팽이관 속에서 되살아나는

Figure of Wind

Wind's fingertip
Every time brushing cliff
Hearing strings bounce

Groping with fingertip
Like groove of LP record
Feeling waves of many patterns

Calling to souls left earth
Wind's playing plucking thousands and millions times
As if leaving bloodstain on fingertip.
Did dig hole in rock?

When breath of lives gather
In valleys and rocks, everywhere
Grooves of Qi waves will shape

Deep in canyons of time.
In bedrock fossil of seaweed
in ammonite shell of fault

If ache like digging heart
Reviving in cochlea

아득한 원생原生의 소리 들을 수 있겠지

창세의 하늘부터
언제나 그 자리에
별들의 자리 새김에서
저들끼리의 당김의 결을
저들의 신화를

지상의 모든 소리가 소멸하고
알파파[1] 쓰나미파[2] 흐르는
삼경三更의 한 찰라에서
별자리 사이

바람의 결
별빛으로 송신하는 기파를
천문泉門의 수상돌기로 감지한다.

1). 뇌의 각성 상태 중에서 비교적 이완된 뇌파로 눈을 감으면 특히 두드러진다.
2). 우주의 이온화 가스물질인 플라즈마를 종을 울리듯 진동하여 만드는 우주파.

Might hear distant sound of primordial life

From heaven of creation
Always in its place
In stars' carving of being
Waves of their pull
Their myth

All sounds of earth are extinguished
Alpha wave[1] tsunami wave[2] flowing
In one moment of samkyeong[3]
Between constellations

Wave of wind
Qi waves transmitted by starlight
Detecting with the dendrites of fontanel

    1). Relatively relaxed brain waves in the wakeful state of the brain, especially noticeable when the eyes are closed.
    2). Cosmic waves that cause the ionised gaseous matter of the universe, plasma, to vibrate like a bell.
    3). The period between eleven o'clock at night and one o'clock in the morning. (Translator's note)

별빛의 화법

별들은 왜 서로
태어나자마자 도망치듯
아득히 멀어져 가는가?

별들이 달려가며 만드는
수천억 광년, 빛 마디들
은하의 물결로 흐른다

별들을 떠나는 기파들
기약 없이 아득히 멀어져 가는 것은

먼 어둠 너머에서
거부할 수 없는
공명의 불빛 때문이다

사무침으로 보내는
흩어진 혼들의 재회를 위한
SOS 모스 신호이다

간절한 중력파[1]를 따라
별들의 기파들, 화이트홀[2] 너머로
양자도약[3]으로, 물질의 틀을 벗어나
영성우주의 시공으로 건너갈거야

Narration of Starlight

Why stars,
As soon as born, seem to flee from each other,
Fading into distance?

Zillions of light years,
Light nodes made by stars as run,
Flowing in galaxy waves

Qi waves leaving stars
Fading away without promise

Beyond distant darkness
Irresistible
Because of resonant light

Sending with deep longing
For reunion of scattered souls
Sos morse signal

Along eager gravitational waves[1]
Stellar Qi waves, beyond white hole[2].
By quantum jump[3], out of material frame
Will cross over to space−time of spiritual universe

지금, 이 별자리에 머무는
얼마 남지 않은 견습기간
천문泉門의 가지돌기를 세우고
별들의 신화를 들을 수 있는
영성 화법에 익숙해져야지.

    1). 시공간(space time) 자체의 뒤틀림을 통해 전파되어 가는 중력(gravitational force)의 주기적인 변화. 질량을 가진 물체가 진동하면 주위 진공에서 중력파가 발생한다.
    2). 블랙홀의 대척점에 있다고. 이론적으로 가상되는 강한 빛과 물질을 방출하는 영역.
    3). 영성 파동. 양자역학적으로 시공간을 초월하는 비국소적 양자기억 정보의 전이.

Now, remaining in this constellation
Few apprentice duration
Setting up dendrites of fontanel
Hearing myths of stars.
Become familiar with spiritual narration.

    1). Periodic changes in the gravitational force propagated through the warping of space–time itself. When an object with mass vibrates, it generates gravitational waves in the surrounding vacuum.
    2). The opposite of a black hole. A theoretical hypothetical region that emits intense light and matter.
    3). Spiritual waves. A non–local transmission of quantum memory information that transcends space and time.

바오밥 채널

마다가스카르 모론다바,
그곳의 바오밥 군락지에 가면
고압전선 아래에 선듯
머리카락이 주뼛주뼛 일어선다

닫쳤던 천문이 다시 열리고
안테나처럼 뻗쳐오른 가지돌기에
어느 행성에서 온 기파가 감지되어
온몸에 전률이 흐른다

일출을 보려고 태백의 정상에서
슬리핑백 속에서 노숙을 하듯,
바오밥 몸통 속에, 수직의 입관을 하는
모론다바의 원주민처럼
서서 입적하듯 들어간다

지상의 모든 주파수를 차단하고
수관 속으로 가지돌기를 밀어올려서
바오밥 군락지가 있는 별들간의 교신을
수십억 광년 너머까지 수신한다

바오밥 채널 속으로 들어온 기파가
초원의 해돋이와 함께 싹을 틔워서

Baobab Channel

Morondava Madagascar,
When go to the baobab colonies there
Like standing under high voltage wires
Hair stands on end

Closed fontanel opening again
By dendrite extending like antennas
Qi waves from some planet are detected
Shiver runs through whole body

At the top of Taebaek[1] to watch sunrise
Like homeless in a sleeping bag,
In body of a baobab, doing vertical ibkoan[2]
Like natives of Morondava
Standing, as if ibjeok[3], going in

Cutting off all earthly frequencies
Pushing dendrite up into water tube
Communications between stars in baobab colonies
Receiving from billions of light years away

Qi waves entering baobab channel
Germinating with sunrise on grassland

정수리 천문을 열고 싹이 솟아오른다
혹성 B 612의 바오밥과도 교신할 수 있는
나의 바오밥 묘목이다

만 미터 고도로 태평양을 건너오며
정수리 위에 새로 개설한 바오밥 채널을
모바일 폰 안테나처럼 테스트해 본다

극동의 아파트 옥상에 바오밥 안테나를 세우고
별빛의 집광으로 밤마다 충전해서
가지돌기 수용체의 고리를 풀고 귀천하는
기체덩이가 공명의 주파수를 감지한다

라이트 세일[4]하는 기류 속에서
시공의 숨결을 되짚어가는 흰연어처럼
영성의 발원지, 그 별자리를 찾아갈 것이다.

1) light sail : 별의 빛에너지로 하는 우주여행.

Opening parietal fontanelle, sprouting shoots
Can communicate with baobab on Planet B612
My baobab seedling

Crossing the Pacific Ocean at an altitude of 10,000 metres
Newly opening baobab channel on crown
Testing like mobile phone antenna

Setting up the baobab antenna on apartment roof in the Far East
Charging nightly with starlight
Unhooking dendrite receptors, returning to Heaven
Gas mass detecting resonant frequency

In air current of light sail[4]
Like white salmon returning to breath of space—time.
Will find the constellation, source of spirituality.

    1) A mountain on the border of Bonghwa-gun, Gyeongsangbuk-do, South Korea, and Taebaek-si, Yeongwol-gun, Gangwon-do, 1,567 metres high. It is known as the 'sacred mountain' of the Taebaek mountain range. (Translator's note)
    2) Placing the body in a coffin. (Translator's note)
    3) A Buddhist term for death, referring to the end of life's suffering and the arrival at a world of quiet joy. (Translator's note)
    4) Travelling through space with the light energy of the stars.

II

컷

간밤의 빗발 속에서
떨어져 나온 방울 하나

전생의 기억인 듯
아직도 반짝이는 새벽별처럼

어둠의 틈새로 번져오는
햇살 속에서 굴러다니다
인연의 한 자락
풀잎 끝에 매달려 있다

꽃잠 든 창을 흔드는 돌바람에
우듬지 둥지 속 새알처럼
아슬아슬 흔들린다

우는 듯, 노래하는 듯
어미 새가 부를 때

익숙한 번지점프를 하듯
수직으로 떨어져
풀섶 그늘 속에 묻힌다.

Cut

In last night's hard rain
A single drop fallen

Like memory from previous life
Like a dawn star still shining

Spreading through darkness
Rolling around in sunshine
A strand of fate
Dangling from a blade of grass

In harsh wind rattling flower—sleeping window
Like bird egg in treetop nest
Dangerously swaying

As if crying, singing
When mother bird calls

Like familiar bungee jump
Falls vertically
Is buried in shade of grass.

바람의 집

  그가 개구리처럼 나의 등에 앉아서 앞발로 몸속의 줄을 뽑아내어
  허공으로 던진다
  일렁이는 헛개나무 가지에 걸쳐지면
  뒷다리에 줄을 묶어 곡예하듯 건너간다

  그가 흙먼지를 일으켜 세웠던 흔적의 집,
  안개를 헤치고 가야 할 무상無相의 집,
  그 사이가 나의 궤도임을 알고 있다
  리프트처럼 흔들리는 그물집이
  내게 주어진 선물이다

  별의 형상으로 태어난 꽃이
  망설임 없이 허공에 몸을 던지고
  씨방 속에서 꿈을 키우듯이,

  내가 던진 수많은 줄들을
  내가 매단 수많은 룽따風馬들을
  둥지 속에서 기억하고 그리워한다

  허공에 걸쳐진 바람의 게르[1]에
  죽어서 내 몸을 그곳에 누이겠지만
  내 혼은 외줄의 허공을 밤마다 몽유할 것이다

House of Wind

He sits on my back like frog
With front paws, pulls threads out of body
Throws into air
When is caught in branches of a fluttering hovenia tree
Ties line to his hind leg, crosses over acrobatically

House of trace he built from dust of earth,
House of nothingness to go through mist,
I know the space between is my orbit
Net swaying like lift
Is Gift given to me

Just as flower born in shape of star
Throwing itself into void without hesitation.
Nurturing dreams in ovary,

Countless ropes my having cast
Countless Qi's horses my tied
Remembering, longing for in nest,

In ger of winds[1] hung in air
Though will die, lay my body there
My soul will wander nightly on air of one rope

그가 부를 때는, 즐거운 몽상의 믿음으로
오늘도 어제처럼 줄을 던진다.

1) 몽골족의 이동식 집.

When he call, with faith of joyful reverie
Throw rope today as yesterday.

1) A mobile house of the Mongols.

가벼움 견습 見習

민들레 씨앗 같은
갓 우화한 저것들

물 위에 내려 앉는다
호수의 수련처럼 뜬다

몸틀이 가벼운 것들,
갈릴리 이적을 보여준다

수상 보드처럼 밀고 가는 파동,
수초들의 그림자가
팔레트 위 수채화 물감처럼 번진다

삽질로 가슴에 고랑을 파듯
바닥의 침전까지 긁어내고
육신의 외피를 얇게 박제한다

기氣가 풍선처럼 부풀리어
보푸라기 날 것처럼 가볍게 떠다니고
파문처럼 번져갈 수 있을까?

탈각,
입자의 골조를 허물고
기파가 탈출 연습을 한다.

Lightness Apprenticeship

Like dandelion seeds
Those freshly unfurled things

Siting down on water
Floating like water lilies in lake

Light body frame
Showing the Galilean miracle.

Waves pushing like water board,
Shadows of water plants
Spreading like watercolour on palette

Like digging furrow in chest with shovel
Scraping away sediment at bottom
Thinly stuffing skin of body

Qi inflating like balloon
Floating lightly as if lint flying
Can spread like ripple?

Dismantling,
Breaking skeleton of particles
Qi waves practicing escape.

밤의 징검다리

자정 무렵
심야 청소차가 지나간 후
인적이 지워져 거리가 깨끗해지면
듬성듬성 남은 빛 조각들이
별자리처럼 얼개를 엮어
징검다리를 만든다

어둠의 농도가 짙어질수록
세포막과 뇌막의 투과성이 높아져서
내 몸과 허공의 삼투압 차이로
혼령이 쉽게 빠져나간다

고공사다리처럼 곧추 선
밤의 징검다리를 건널 때는
불나방의 허물이 되어
몸의 무게를 느끼지 못한다

유체이탈 시
몸속에 남겨둔 혼의 침낭이
물고기 부레처럼 띄워주기 때문일까?

삼족오(三足烏)의 날개가 없어도
빛 조각의 징검다리를 건너서
황천 저편까지 몽유 산책을 하다
동트기 전에 다녀온다.

Setepping Stone of Night

Around midnight
After late-night sweeper passed
When streets are cleared of human traces
Remaining pieces of light here and there
Weaving frame like constellation
Creating setepping stone

As intensity of darkness deepens
Permeability of cell membranes and brain membranes increasing
Due to osmotic pressure difference between my body and air
Spirit easily escaping

When crossing night's stepping stone
Straight as high ladder
Becoming moth's epidermis
Don't feel weight of body

When disembodied
Is it because sleeping bag of soul left in body
Makes float me like fish's bladder?

Even without wings of three-footed crow
Crossing bridge of light shards
Sleepwalking to other side of netherworld
Coming back before dawn.

그림자 무언극

붉은 모래바다 위를
대나무 마디 무늬의 검은 뱀이
나선의 곡선으로 유성처럼 건너간다

그림자놀이를 하는
뱀의 그림자 옆구리에 붙어서
등짐 진 낙타대상이 따라간다

해독할 수 없는 발굽의 행렬 대신
캐터필러 문양의 그림자가 사막의 영토에서는
바람에 지워지지 않는 소통의 주역이 된다

건기에 자주 굳어버리는 혀의 활판 대신에
그림자 토막들의 행렬 영상이
그림자 무언극의 상형문자 자막을 보여준다

한 번도 악기 소리에 담아보지 않은 음률들이
사구 골짜기에 가득 고인 그림자 호수에서
선사先史의 흑백 정경 신기루를 바라보며
원시의 알몸으로 유영해 본다

베두인 유목인들이 장거리 사막횡단 여행에서
그림자 오아시스에서 안식을 구하듯이,

Shadow Pantomime

On sea of red sand
Black snake with bamboo node patterns
Crossing like meteor in spiral curve

Shadow—playing
Clinging to shadowed flank of snake
Burdened camel following

Instead of procession of indecipherable hooves
Shadows of caterpillar's pattern in desert territory
Becoming symbol of communication unerasble by wind

Instead of tongue's typography often hardened in dry season
Procession images of shadow parts
Showing hieroglyphic subtitles of pantomime

Notes, never carried in sound of instrument
In lake of shadows pooling in dune valley
As gazing at mirage of prehistoric black—white scene
Swimming in pristine nakedness

Bedouin nomads on long desert crossing journey
As if seeking rest in shadow oases,

영성 기파와의 주파수 공명을 위해
별자리 무대 위의 그림자놀이로
유체이탈의 예행연습을 한다.

For frequency resonance in spiritual Qi waves
With shadow play on constellation stage
Rehearsing for out—of—body.

밤낚시 2

달의 중력이 가냘퍼지는
그믐달 밤,

지느러미가 날개되어
별을 탐하는 천어天魚를 본다

강가의 암벽에 그려진
고래 이빨 바늘에 꿰인
전설의 조어鳥魚이다

대곡리 어부들
통나무배를 타고 나간다

달과 샛별을 바라보며
경문經文의 주술을 미끼밥으로 던진다

그믐달 바늘에 미끼를 꿰고
오색 룽따風馬의 찌를 달아
별자리 수초 사이로 낚싯대를 드리운다

몽유의 포인트를 옮겨 다녀도
새벽이 되도록 채우지 못한다

빈칸에 멈춰 선 펜촉처럼

Night Fishing 2

Moon's gravity is fading
Night of the old moon,

With fins winged
Seeing sky-fish hungry for star

Painted on rocks by river
Needled with whale teeth
Is legendary bird-fish

Daegokri[1] fishermen
Going out on dugouts

As gazing at moon and venus
Casting spells of Buddhist scriptures as bait

Threading bait through needle of old moon
With hook of five-colored Qi's horse
Casting rod through constellation water plants

Though moving among points of reverie
Can't fill it to dawn

Like nip stopping at blank space

빈 낚싯바늘만 목젖처럼
동트는 수평선에 걸려있다

희미해져 가는
그믐달의 뒤꿈치를 바라본다

빈 망태를 말아 안고
금식 안거에 들어가는
늙은 달팽이

샛별이 힐끗 쳐다본다.

Only empty fishhook like uvula
Hanging on horizon at dawn

Fading away
Looking at heel of the fading moon

Roll up empty mesh bag
Entering fasting retreat
Old snail

Morning star glancing.

    1). Daegok-ri, Eonyang-eup, Ulju-gun, Ulsan-si, South Korea, home of the national treasure Petroglyphs of Bangudae Terrace. There are the oldest whale hunting petroglyphs in the world. (Translator's note)

천등제 天燈祭

어둠의 농도가 짙어질수록

간절함으로 가슴벽을 긁을수록
통절함으로 가슴벽을 칠수록
가슴팍이 붉게 멍이 든다

피는 인화성 강한 기름이 되고
심장판막이 부싯돌로 부딪혀서
심지에 불꽃이 피어나서
심장은 불항아리로 달구어진다

일생을 허기진 듯 숨가쁘게 살아온
고산高山의 적혈구과다증 사람들이
통성기도 하며 사혈의 등燈을
하늘에 띄워 올린다

염원의 열기가 궁륭에 닿아
불항아리 속 붉은피톨들이 뿜어져 나와
신생의 별들이 될 게다

천등에 적힌 글발들은
별자리에 피딱지로 엉겨 붙어
룽다처럼 펄럭이며,

Sky Lantern Festival

As density of darkness deepen

As scratch chest wall with desperation
As bang chest wall with anguish
Chest turning bruised, red

Blood turning into highly flammable oil
Heart valves are strucking with flint
Sparks blooming in wick
Heart heating as fire pot

Lived whole life breathlessly as if starving
Erythrocytosis people in high mountains
With tongseong−gido[1], lanterns of phlebotomy
Raise to sky

Heat of prayer reach to dome of sky
Red blood cells in fire jar will spew out
Become newborn stars.

Letters written on sky lantern
Stucked to constellations as dried bloodstains
While fluttering like Qi horse,

황도 12궁[1]에 대한
별 아이들의 편지가 될 게다.

1) 黃道十二宮: 춘분점이 위치한 물고기자리부터 양자리, 황소자리, 쌍둥이자리, 게자리, 사자자리, 처녀자리, 천칭자리, 전갈자리, 궁수자리, 염소자리, 물병자리의 12 별자리를 말한다.

To 12 signs of zodiac[2]
Will become letters of children like star.

    1) Tongseong-gido is a form of Christian prayer that is said out loud, also known as Korean prayer in English-speaking countries. (Translator's note)
    2) The 12 signs of the zodiac are Pisces, where the equinoxes are located, through Aries, Taurus, Gemini, Cancer, Leo, Virgo, Libra, Scorpio, Sagittarius, Capricorn, and Aquarius.

나의 주소지

시냅스의 고리가 풀려
탈육한 혼령이
한 생의 구역을 벗어나며
잠시 멀리, 지난 삶터를 돌아본다

저, 창백한 덩어리
낙타의 푸른 똥,
검은 사막 위에서
쇠똥구리가 굴리고 가는

줌인하면
똥별에 깊이 패인 중앙 계곡,
그 양쪽의 푸른 구릉의 초원

브로카 영역에서 꿈틀거리는 식물성 양 떼
브로드만 영역을 폭주하는
송곳니의 광물성 맹수들

조금 더 줌인하면
가지돌기의 이랑들 사이
수액으로 질척이는 고랑들 속에서

성충의 꿈을 꾸는 구더기처럼

My Address

Synaptic ring loosening,
Disembodying spirit
Leaving confines of one life,
For a while, looking back on the distant past of life.

That, pale lump
Blue dung of camel,
On black desert
Dung beetle rolling, going

Zooming in
Central valley deeply gouged by shooting star,
Green hilly grasslands on both sides

Vegetable sheeps wriggling in Brocca area
Rampaging through Brodman realm
Fanged mineralized beasts

Zooming in a little further
Between ridges of dendrite
In sludgy furrows with sap

Like maggot dreaming of imago

허우적거리는 바이러스들,
악성세포로 변종하다, 킬러세포에 의해
살처분 되는 바이러스들,
악몽과 몽유의 기압골에 갇혀
자폭하는 바이러스들,

쓰나미파로 몰려오는
고투와 신음의 파동들,
도망치듯 다시 줌아웃하면

저, 희미해지는 한 생의
서럽고 아린, 창백하고 푸른
기억 한 덩어리여!

Floundering viruses,
While mutate into malignant cell, by killer cells
Viruses to be destroyed,
Trapped in trough of nightmare and daydream
Self-destructing viruses,

Rushing in tsunami wave,
Waves of struggle and moan,
Zooming out again like a fugitive

That, fading away, a life's
Sad spreathed, pale blue
A lump of memory!

의자의 회상

폐가의 뒤편 묵정밭에
녹슨 의자 하나가 있다

곁의 사과나무 가지에
땀에 절은 모자가 걸려있고
십자형 말뚝에
기름때 묻은 셔츠가 걸쳐져 있다

흙투성이 피로에 삭은
육신이 앉았을, 저 의자

그을은 지푸라기가
희끗한 기억의 머리카락처럼
의자 밑에 깔린 노동의 그늘 속에 흩어져 있다

지상의 배추와
지하의 고구마 밭이었을까?

삽질로 출렁거렸던 텃밭 위에서
거룻배처럼 흔들거렸을까?
저 의자

구월의 한낮, 뜨거운 햇볕에

Reminiscence of Chair

In weed—grown fallow behind abandoned house
Is a rusty chair

On branch of nearby apple tree
Salted hat hangs
On crossed stake
Grease—stained shirt hangs

Worn out by muddy fatigue
That chair, where flesh would have sat

Smoke—stained straw
Like hair of faint memory
Scattered in shadow of labor beneath chair

Maybe was cabbage field above ground
And sweet potato underground?

On shaking vegetable garden with shoveling
Swayed like lighter?
That chair

September midday, under scorching sun

화장이 되고만 것일까?

그의 혼령은
휘발성 강한 기파로 증발한 것일까?

사과를 베어 물고 앉았던
달콤한 낮잠의 자리였을 자리,
지금은
집행장의 의자처럼 적막하다.

Just cremated?

His spirit
Evaporated as volatile Qi wave?

Sat, biting into an apple
Could have been seat of sweet nap.
Now
Is quiet like chair in execution place.

환상통 날개

어깻죽지에 환상통을 앓아오던
한 사내가, 절벽의 어린 도요새처럼
양팔을 펼치고 고층 빌딩에서 점프했다

이륙 직후 비행에 실패한 새끼 도요새처럼 추락했다

그림자 날개를 드리우고 누운 플라타너스 낙엽처럼
양쪽 겨드랑이에서 흘러나온 피가
땅바닥에서 검은 날개를 펼쳤다

수많은 번지점프의 예행연습 덕분인지
그의 얼굴 표정은 안온했다

언제나 미소를 지으며 동네거리를 걸어 다니던 그,
가끔씩 하늘을 쳐다보고. 독백처럼 아버지를 불렀다

옷은 남루했지만 긴 머리의 얼굴은 잘 생긴 배우 같았다
슈퍼스타 주인공, 그가 부활한 것일까?

지붕 위에 솟구친 수많은 십자가들
창문을 흔드는 수많은 기도와 찬송들
서가에 갇힌 수많은 말씀의 경전들

아직은 뜻이 땅에서는 이루어지지 못한 탓일까?

Phantom Pain Wings

Man suffering phantom pain in shoulder blades
Like young snipe on cliff
Spreading arms, jumping from skyscraper

Falling like chick snipe failed right after takeoff

Like platan leaf lying with shadowy wings,
Blood oozing from both armpits,
Spreading black wings on ground

As if practiced many bungee jumps
His face expression was calm

He, always smiling, walking down village street
Often looked up at sky, like monologue, called father

Clothes shabby, but long hair's face was like
handsome actor
  Superstar protagonist, maybe is resurrected?

Many crosses soaring over roofs
Countless prayers and hymns shaking window
Countless scriptures of the word locked in shelve

Because will had not yet done on earth?

하늘이, 그의 눈처럼 청명한 날
허물을 벗어 놓은 듯
땅위에 꿈의 날개만 펼쳐놓고
마치 자살처럼 귀천했다

그 빌딩 위로 떠가는
그가 아파하던 환상 날개가 보이고
비둘기 친구에게 먹이를 주던
그의 부드러운 목소리가
손바닥에 닿는다.

The sky, clear day as his eyes
As if sloughed
Spreading only dream's wings on earth
Returned to sky like suicide

He, floating away over building
Seeing illusionary wings of his pain
Feeding pigeon friend
His soft voice
Touching palm.

춘인 春印

봄눈 녹아 질펀해진 햇볕 속에서
들녘 수로의 혈액세포들이 펄떡인다

시원의 원형질 그대로
억년의 시간 동안 품고 있는
늪지의 체세포들도
웅크렸던 손바닥을 편다

홍매화 화인花印을 찍는 꽃비가
춘몽 속 방언으로 흩날린다

괴성에 뛰쳐나온 개구리들이
달빛 흥건한 창살 문 빈칸마다
자동기술하듯 알을 쏟아놓는다

늙은 몽춘기夢春期의 나도
홍역의 뇌 후유증으로 넋두리하듯
꽃물 몽정을 불면의 요 위에 쏟아내어

봄밤의 달무리를 그린다.

Spring Stamp

In sloppy sunlight, spring snow melting
Blood cells of field waterway pulsating

As the original protoplasm
Holding for billion years
Also swamp's body cells
Straighting clenched palms

Flower rain stamping red plum figures
Fluttering as tongues in spring dreams

Frogs leaping out at shout
Every blank in grating bathed in moonlight
Like automatism, pouring out eggs

Old spring dreams, puberty's me too
Like gibberish from cerebral aftereffects of measles
Spilling flowery wet dream over sleepless sheets

Painting moon halo on spring night.

안단테 칸타빌레[1]

초승달로 돋아나서
잠자는 호수의 등을 밟고 가듯이
수초의 달그림자를 딛고 갈 거야

긴 여름 여문 해바라기 씨알
한 톨 한 톨, 들길에 뿌려놓고
깨금발로 되새기며 걸어갈 거야

동백이나 목련처럼
부푼 가슴살, 단칼에 도려내지 않고

달맞이꽃 봉오리, 차오르고 이울어지듯이
한 달에 한 잎, 백 년을 걸려서 떨어질 거야

달빛에 삭은 벼랑의 소나무,
천궁처럼 등뼈 휘어지게 하듯

밤마다 석별의 가슴앓이로
촛불처럼 조금씩, 사위어져 갈 거야

정선아리랑 실은 동강의 거룻배,
첼로 활의 안단테 보폭으로
달빛 잠방이며, 강을 건너갈 거야

Andante Cantabile[1]

Sprouting into a crescent moon
As if stepping on back of sleeping lake
Will walk on moon shadow of water plants

Sunflower kernel in long summer
One by one, scattering on field path
On tiptoe, ruminating, will walk along

Like camellia or magnolia
Buffy breast, not cut by a single slash

Evening primrose bud, like filling, tilting
One leaf a month, want to take a hundred years to fall

Pines on cliff, faded in moonlight,
As if spine bending like god's bow

With heartache of parting every night
Like candle, little by little, will fade away

Rowboat on the Dong-gang River[2] carrying Jeongseon-Arirang[3],
With andante stride of cello bow

그믐달 실눈, 한 올만 남을 때까지
한 겹 한 겹. 천천히 야위어 가듯이

극락강 건너가는 솜털 구름처럼
노을의 바람에 실려, 안단테 아니,
레퀴엠의 아다지오 보폭으로
되돌아보며, 뒷걸음으로 떠나갈 거야.

1) "천천히 노래하듯이" 라는 음악용어이며, 러시아의 작곡가 차이코프스키의 『현악4중주곡 제1번 D 장조』(작품번호 11)의 제2악장이기도 하다.

Will cross river, dabbling in moonlight

Fine eyes of old moon, until only one strand remains
Layer by layer. As if slowly disappearing

Like fluff cloud crossing paradise river
Carried by wind in sunset, andante no,
With adagio stride of requiem
Looking back, will leave backwards.

> 1) It is a musical term "as if singing slowly" and is also the second movement of Russian composer Tchaikovsky's String Quartet No. 1 in D Major (Work No. 11).
> 2) The river that runs from Gasu−ri, south of Jeongseon−eup, Jeongseon−gun, Gangwon−do, to Yeongwol−gun. Many limestone caves and rocky cliffs, combined with fall foliage, make up one of Korea's most beautiful scenic spots. (Translator's note)
> 3) The traditional local folk song from Jeongseon, Gangwon−do, South Korea, sung by a group of people taking turns. (Translator's note)

젖은 첼로

안개의 주정酒精을 밤새 마셔
만취된 깃털의 날개로
심해어처럼 유영한다

심저의 음자리 C2 현 위로
안단테의 보폭으로

흉통을 움켜쥔 손으로
아프게 두드려도
두드려도 열어주지 않던
심장의 방문들을 이제사
모두 열어 보인다

손금처럼 잔잔히 갈라지는
거울 검색대 위에
검은 피톨들, 엉킨 피딱지들을
모두 내어 놓는다

텅 비어버린 울림통의 결을
바람의 손끝이 짚어가며 소리를 낸다

어릴 때, 귓불을 만져주던 우물 속 울림 같은

Wet cello

Drinking ethanol of fog all night long
With wings of drunken feathers
Swimming like deep sea fish

Above C2 note string, in deep heart
With andante stride

With hand clutching chest pain
Even when knocked, painfully
Never opened
Heart's doors just now
All opening, showing

On the mirror's reflective table
Gently splitting like palm lines
Black blood particles, tangled scabs
All are exposed

Wave of empty resonating box
Wind's fingertips tracing, making sound

As child, sound of well touching earlobes

태아 때, 알몸을 휘감아주던 양수 속 해조 같은
혼령 때, 춤사위로 흐르던 파동 속 율려律呂 같은

As fetus, like algae in amniotic fluid wrapping around naked body
As spirit, like Yullyeo[1] in waves flowing as dance moving

1) Yullyeo: the source of life and the creative spirit from which all things in the universe are born, the ground from which the infinite harmony of the universe arises. (Translator's note)

흙

새들의 깃털과
물고기들의 살과
짐승들의 뼈,
그것들의 반죽인 것이라

그 한 움큼
쇠똥구리가 한나절
굴리고 가는, 찐득찐득한
살가루 흙 주먹밥 아닌가

그 한 자락
다람쥐가 한겨울
감싸고 자는, 보송보송한
털가루 흙 모포 아닌가

그 한 덩어리
도공이 한 생을
달빛으로 빚으니
바람의 기를 담은
뼛가루 흙 항아리 아닌가

그 한 가닥
향으로 말아 올리니
한 생의 잠이
꿈으로 향기롭더라.

Soil

Feathers of birds
Flesh of fishes
Bones of beasts,
Be dough of them

That one handful
Dung beetle's day
Rolling, sticky
Isn't flesh—dust, earth—rice balls

That one patch
Squirrel, in midwinter
Curlling up, sleeping, cozy
Isn't blanket of earth, fur dust

That one lump
Potter's whole life
Shaping with moonlight;
Containing wind's Qi
Isn't clay jar holding bone dust

That one strand
Rolled up in incense;
Lifetime's slumber
Such a fragrant dream

흉터

몸체의 흉터를 보면
무너진 옛 토성과 성채의 잔해가 생각난다

그 퇴색과 일그러짐을 보고
슬픔의 깊이와 통증의 강도를
고고학적으로 유추해 본다

얼굴의 흉터를 보면
탈선의 긁힘과 균열,
모서리가 떨어져 나간
오래된 LP 판이 생각난다

그 거친 숨소리와 쉰 목소리,
사실과 진실의 어긋난 간격을
음성학적으로 유추해 본다.

그의 뒷모습의 길이와
밟고 선 그림자 두께를 보며
은폐된 내상을 기하학적으로 측량해본다

별들이 희미하게 보여주는
분화구의 병력을 망원 렌즈로 보며
오래된 상처의 생성과 변화를

Scar

Observing at a scar on body
Reminded of ruins of ancient saturn and citadel collapsed

By looking at fading and distortion
Depth of sorrow and intensity of pain
Infering archaeologically

Looking at facial scar
Scratche and crack of derailment,
With corner peeling off
Reminding of old LP record

The ragged breathing and hoarse voice,
Dislocated gap between fact and truth
Phonetically inferring

Looking at length of his backside and
Thickness of shadow stepped on
Geometrically measuring concealed internal injury

Stars faintly showing
Observing crater's disease history through telescopic lens
Formation and change of old wound

점성학적으로 유추해본다.

눈빛의 떨림과 젖은 굴절을 보면서
그의 자학과 원망을 어루만져 줄
기호를 언어학적으로 검색해 본다.

Astrologically analogizing.

Watching tremor and wet refraction of eyes
Will soothe his self−torment and resentment
Searching linguistically for sign.

III

1.0.

1.

나무 하나가
건기의 들소처럼 선채
잎을, 껍질을
흰 뼈가 드러나도록
바람에 뜯기고 있다

들소 하나가
흑단나무처럼 선채
살점을, 소리를
초원의 바람이 붉게 젖도록
사자에게 뜯기고 있다

0.

피톨들,
바위 위 빗방울처럼
기억들,
구름 위 깃털처럼
흩어지고 있다

1.0.

1.

A single tree
Standing like buffalo in dry season
Leaves and bark
Till white bones are exposed
Bited by wind

One buffalo
Standing like ebony tree
Flesh, sound
Untill winds of prairie soaks red
Bited by lion

0.

Blood-particles,
Like raindrop on rock
Memories,
Like feathers on cloud
Scattering

한 조각의 공간이 어둠 속에 닫히고
한 토막의 시간이 고요 속에 묻히고 있다

마지막
한 가닥 빛살이
한 가락 파동이
블랙다이아몬드 같은 진공의 알 속으로
빨려 들어가고 있다.

A piece of space closing in darkness
A piece of time being entombed in silence

The last
A single light
A single wave
Into egg of vacuum like black diamond
Being sucked.

뻘길

여자만 갯벌에
핏줄로 뻗어가는 붉은 길

자궁 내막에 뿌리내린
탯줄 같은 뻘길을 따라

몽당다리로 뒤뚱거리는
갓 태어난 거북이처럼
배지느러미 다리로
껑충거리는 망둥이처럼

먼 바다에서 불어오는
아득한 내음
모유의 기억을 쫓아서

맨발로 달려가는
돌잡이 알몸이 되어
젖가슴 속에 들어가리라.

Muddy Road

On the yeojaman bay[1] foreshore
Red road running through vessel

Rooted in endometrium
Along muddy road, like umbilical cord

Staggering on stubby legs
Like newborn turtle
With ventral fin legs
Like goby floundering

Blowing in from distant sea
Distant scent
Chasing memory of mother's milk

Running barefoot
Doljabi[2] naked
Will return to mom's breast.

> 1) A bay on the south coast of South Korea, located in the central-western part of the country, with a huge reed bed and widely recognized internationally as a wintering ground and habitat for rare birds. (Translator's note)
> 2) A child at his first birthday. (Translator's note)

겨울 등정

눈 내린 겨울산은
출입통제구역이다

불립문자의 겨울나무들이
긴 차단기를 등성이에 걸쳐놓고
수문장처럼 눈을 부라리며 막아선다

무단 입산하려는 나를 향해
칼바람소리를 지르며
가지돌기 회초리를 휘두른다

마른 꽃가지를 움켜쥐어 부러뜨린 팔이 잘린다
흰 속살에 아이젠의 흉터를 파놓은 다리가 잘린다

토르소가 되어 주저앉아 있는 나를
까치가 나무에서 내려다 본다

눈 내린 능선의 밤에 엎드려
파충류가 시조새로 진화하듯이
견갑골이 날개가 되는 꿈을 꾼다.

Winter climbing

Snowy winter mountain
Off—limits

Winter trees of unreadable script
Stretch long barriers across ridge
Like gatekeeper chief, glaring, blocking way.

Toward me entering without permission
Screaming in knife—wind
Brandishing dendrite whip

Arm cutting off, broken by clutching dried flower branch
Leg cutting off, dug scar with crampon in white flesh

Me crouching like torso
Magpie looking down from tree

Prostrating in night of snowy ridge
As if reptile evolving into archaeopteryx
Dreaming of shoulder blade becoming wings.

천산(天山)으로 가는길

할아버지의 할아버지들이 넘어간 발자국들을 되짚으며
지상의 우듬지들을 까마득히 바라보았다

호모 에렉투스[1], 킬리만자로산(Mt. Kilimanjaro)을 바라보며
등뼈를 곧추세우고, 앞발의 자유를 얻었다

호모 사피엔스[2], 사하라(Sahara) 초원을 건너서
옐부르스(Elbrus) 영봉을 비추는 아침 해를 바라보며
지혜의 빛을 전두前頭에 담았다

퇴화된 등뼈 지르러미와 견갑골 날개의
스멀거리는 기억을 되새기며
크로노스(Kronos)의 숨소리처럼 멈추지 않고 걸었다

천산의 깊은 그늘에서 불어오는
그윽한 신성의 바람결에 잠시 걸음을 멈추었다

아버지의 아버지들은 타림분지에서
바이칼바람꽃들이 만년을 읊조리는
끝없는 전설의 꽃길을 만들었다

동쪽의 끝, 아침 해의 땅을 향해

Road to Sky Mountain

As retracing footsteps of grandfather's foregrandfathers
Looking far away at treetops of earth

Homo erectus[1], gazing at Mt. Kilimanjaro
Straightening backbone, freeing forefoot

Homo sapiens[2], crossing the Sahara steppe
As looking at morning sun shining on Elbrus peak
Holding light of wisdom in the frontal lobe

Degenerated dorsal fins and scapular wings
Ruminating on memories wriggling
Walking without stopping like breathing sound of Kronos

Blowing from deep shadows of sky mountain
Stopping for a while on secret wind of divine

Father's forefathers in the Tarim Basin
Baikal windflowers reciting for ten thousand years
Creating endless trail of legendary flowers

Toward end of east, land of morning sun

고비(Gobi)의 모래와 송화松花의 강물을 건너
태백산맥에 오른 호모 스페이스쿠스[3]

천제단에서 정수리 천문泉門을 열고
접신 의식을 올리며
별자리들의 신화를 듣고
별빛의 주파수 공명을 느꼈다

암벽 능선에 이생의 뼈를 묻는
히말라야의 마코르(markhor)처럼,
만년설 속에 혼의 깃털을 묻는
타지크(Tajik)의 검독수리처럼
천산 산맥의 능선에 오르리라

천문의 수상돌기 기파가
시공간으로 직방으로 도약하여
종착지 천산의 게이트(gate)에 닿으리라

한 뭉치의 기파로 피어올라
은하를 따라, 쓰나미파[4]를 따라
먼 영성여행을 하리라.

---

    1) homo erectus
    2) homo sapience
    3) homo spacecus
    4) 성간 우주(interstellar space)에서 이온화된 가스물질인 플라즈마가 종처럼 진동하여 만들어지는 우주의 소리.

Acrossing the Gobi sands and the Songhua river
Homo spacecus[3] climbing the Taebaek Mountains

Opening parietal fontanel at Heavenly Altar[4]
Holding a ceremony receiving deity
Listening to mythology of constellations
Feeling frequency resonance of starlight

Burying bones of this life on rocky ridge
Like markhor in the Himalayas,
Burying spiritual feathers in ice cap
Like Tajik black eagle
Will climbing ridges of the Tianshan Mountains

Fontanelle's dendrites, Qi waves
Leaping straight through space time
Reaching gate of sky mountain

Rising as a bundle of Qi waves
Along galaxy, along tsunami waves[5]
Will taking distant spiritual journey.

    1) homo erectus.
    2) homo sapience.
    3) homo spacecus.
    4) An altar set up by the ancients to perform sacrifices in the sky, said to have been built during the time of Dangun, the ancestor of the Korean people. (Translator's note)
    5) A cosmic sound made by ionized gaseous matter, plasma, vibrating like a bell in interstellar space.

믿음의 뿌리

아득한 옛날, 유라시아 대평원에서
에렉투스, 하이델베르크, 네안데르탈, 데니소바, 사피엔스
지층의 오색 띠처럼 함께 살았다

대홍수 때 배를 타고
파미르고원, 천산산맥, 알타이산맥, 티베트고원에서
구원의 부락을 세우고 함께 살았다

태양의 족속 동이는 동쪽으로 가서, 환인 하느님을 섬기고
천산의 천제단에서 올리는 기도의 말
천부경 속에 내려받은 하늘의 뜻
말씀의 뿌리가 동녘 끝까지 뻗어갔다

만년의 시간, 하늘 산을 넘으며
요하 유역과 동북평원에서, 텡그리[1] 나라를 세웠다

영육의 기가 약해질 때마다, 하느님을 불렀다
시련이 생길 때마다, 잘못을 저지를 때마다
어여삐 용서하실 때마다, 믿음의 뿌리는 깊어갔다

양과 음의 손을 깍지 끼고
소망의 기파는 창생의 말씀처럼
땅과 마음속 어디엔들

Roots of Faith

    Long ago, on the Eurasian steppe
    Erectus, Heidelberg, Neanderthal, Denisova, Homo sapiens
    Lived together like five-colored bands of stratum

    In boats during the great flood
    In the Pamirs, the Tianshan Mountains, the Altai Mountains, the Tibetan Plateau
    Built village of salvation, lived together

    Tribe of sun, Dongi[1] went to the east, served the God Whoan-in[2]
    Words of prayer from Cheonjaedan[3] of Sky Mountain
    Will of heaven sent down from the Chunbu-kyung[4]
    Root of the Word stretched out to end of the east

    Time of ten thousand years, Crossing over Sky mountain
    In the Raohe River Basin and the Northeast Plain, established the nation of Tengri[5]

    Whenever Qi of spirit and body weakened, called upon God
    Whenever trials arose, whenever made mistake
    Each time forgave kindly, root of faith deepened

씨알이 뿌려지고, 뿌리가 닿을 수 있었다.

1)tengri : 고대 튀르크어에서 유래했으며, 하느님, 신을 뜻한다.

With hands crossed between positive and negative
Like the Word of creation, Qi wave of hope
Anywhere in earth and heart
Seeds sprinkled, Root could reach.

> 1) A term used to refer to our people, including the tribes that lived eastward of ancient China. (Translator's note)
> 2) A sky god in the myth of Dangun, the founding myth of the Korean people. (Translator's note)
> 3) An altar set up by the ancients to perform sacrifices in the sky, said to have been built during the time of Dangun, the ancestor of the Korean people. (Translator's note)
> 4) An 81-character poem written by an ancient ancestor of the Korean people on the rock wall of Myohyangsan Mountain describing the creation of the universe. It depicts the infinite repetition of the three poles of heaven, earth, and man as math from 1 to 10. It is the principle of moving from one to three and from three to one. (Translator's note)
> 5) Originated from the ancient Turkic language, it means God, the Lord.

풍장

10월의 해바라기처럼 태울 것이다
11월의 솔방울처럼 비울 것이다
12월의 장미처럼 버릴 것이다

대관령의 황태처럼 몸통을 말릴 것이다
원대리의 자작나무처럼 뼈를 말릴 것이다
까치밥으로 매달린 단감처럼 심장을 말릴 것이다
바위 틈 사이 호두처럼 골수를 말릴 것이다

눈물, 산정의 마코르[1] 속눈썹 사이로
붉은피톨, 숭숭한 골다공 사이로
꿈결, 앙상한 가지돌기 사이로

빠져나가
흰 구름 위로 날아갈 것이다

탈육한 흰나비 떼들,
바람의 결을 타고
어디, 아득한 허공 저편

별들의 굴속에 홀씨로 묻히려나.

Aerial Sepulture

Will burn like sunflowers in October
Will empty like pinecone in November
Will throw away like rose in December

Will dry body like dried pollacks of Daegwanryeong[1]
Will dry bones like birch of Wondae-ri[2]
Will dry heart like persimmon hanging for ggachibab[3]
Will dry marrow like walnut between rocks

Tears, markhor[4] on mountain peak, between eyelashes.
Red cell, through perforated bone
In dream, through haggard dendrites

Escaping
Will fly above white cloud

Shedding white butterflies
Riding wind wave
Where, faraway beyond midair

Will buried as spore in cavern of stars.

1) 아프가니스탄, 히말라야, 티베트의 산악 지대에 주로 사는 솟과에 속한 포유동물.

1) It is a ridge connecting Daegwallyeong-myeon, Pyeongchang-gun, Gangwon-do, South Korea, and Seongsan-myeon, Gangneung-si, and is 832 meters high. It is also famous for producing the dried pollack. (Translator's note)

2) A place name in Inje-eup, Inje-gun, Gangwon-do, South Korea, a tourist destination famous for its birch forests. (Translator's note)

3) A persimmon that is often left unpicked as food for flying birds such as magpies. (Translator's note)

4) A mammal of the cattle family that lives mainly in the mountainous regions of Afghanistan, the Himalayas, and Tibet.

하모니카 주법으로

우리의 합주는
하모니카 주법으로 한다

허파꽈리를 입속에서 터뜨려
속알갱이를 목구멍 속으로 불어 넣어주면
꽃물 속에 빠진 붉은가슴벌새
날개 파닥이는 소리가 난다

아침 나팔꽃처럼 내민
꽃술을 빨아먹으면
취기에 물구나무선 꿀벌
꽁지에서 바람개비 소리가 난다

한 탄광마을에서 사는
규폐증 환자끼리 하는
양방향 심폐소생술이다

With harmonica technique

Our ensemble
playing in harmonica style

Bursting alveola in the mouth
Blowing granules into the throat
Red—chest hummingbirds falling into flower nectar
Make flapping wings sound

Sucking stamen
Sticking out like morning glory
Bee drinking, standing on head
Making pinwheel sound from butt

Is a two—way CPR technique
Practiced by silicosis patients
In a mining town.

죽록원 소요 逍遙

새벽 발기한 대나무 숲길을 걷는다

대나무의 사타구니 사이로
포피를 뚫고 솟구쳐 올라가는
팔뚝만 한 죽순들

그 탱탱한 촉감을 발바닥으로 느껴본다

머리 위에서
폭포로 쏟아지는
댓잎의 징 소리
혼미한 이마를 두들긴다

수련의 녹즙이 흐르는
조곤조곤한 뿌리의 소리
양말을 벗고 발을 씻는다

대나무 숲속을 맨발로 걸으며
공기청정기의 필터를 교체한다
허파꽈리의 먼지를 털어낸다

폐엽이 날개를 펼치고

Bamboo Forest Ramble

Walking through upright bamboo forest at dawn

Through groin of bamboo
Sprouting up through foreskin
Bamboo shoots as big as forearm

Feeling springy tactile sensation beneath soles

Overhead
Pouring down like waterfall
Sound of gong from bamboo leaves
Pounding forehead in confusion

Flowing green juice of water lily
Sound of quiet roots
Taking off socks, washing feet

Walking barefoot in bamboo forest
Changing filter in air cleaner
Brushing off dust of alveolas

Lung lobes spreading wings

물고기 부레로 부푼다

풍선 인형이 되어, 넘실넘실
댓잎 구름 위로 걸어본다.

Swelling like fish bladder

Becoming balloon doll, bobbing lightly
Walking on clouds of bamboo leaves

화석의 꿈

시간을 순간 응고시킨
억년의 석회물, 압축 슬라이드를
전자현미경으로
그 기억의 절편을 들여다 본다

지판의 침대 위에 암모나이트가
나선의 미이라로 누워있다
빛의 손끝으로 더듬어보는 무늬의 결
고생대의 문자로 변형시켜본다

억 년의 씨앗에서 싹이 돋아나듯이
화석입자를 깨치고 나오는 공룡의 울음

견고한 석관의 눈꺼풀이 열리고
말랑말랑해진 암모나이트의 기억이
외계의 우주음처럼 녹아나온다

아득한 시간의 단층 속에서
잠수병에 걸린 암모나이트처럼
일상의 지판 속에서 늙고 병들어
더 이상 견디기 힘들어 지는 날

수마트라 섬, 시나붕 산정

Dream of Fossil

Coagulated time in a moment
Billion years of calcification, compressed slide
With an electron microscope
Peering into fragment of that memory

On bed of earth plate, ammonite
Lying to be spiral mummy
Pattern wave groping with fingertip of light
Transforming into letter of the Paleozoic

Sprouting from billion years' seed
Dinosaur cry breaking through fossilized particle

Eyelids of solid sarcophagus opening
Memories of soft ammonites
Dissolving like alien cosmic sound

In fault of distant time.
Like ammonite with caisson disease
Old and diseased in earth plate of everyday
Day not bearing anymore

Atop Mount Sinabung, Sumatra

화산재 쏟아지는 그곳에 알몸으로 누우면
해마 핵 속의 들끓는 기억의 입자들이
화산재 석회물로 순간 응고되어
암모나이트처럼 입관되겠지

혼돈의 억년을 암반 속에서
화석 지판의 슬라이드가 되어 견디면
억 년 후 어느 AI 전자현미경이
호모사피엔스 화석의 비문을 해독하겠지

화석이 된 시상[1]의 꿈도 감지해 낼 수 있을까?

1) 시상(視床, Thalamus): 대뇌의 안쪽, 중뇌의 바로 전측 및 배측에 놓여있으며, 대뇌피질에 투사되는 주요 감각계의 최종 중계소다.

Lying naked there in pouring ash
Boiling-up particles of memory in hippocampal
nucleus
Instantly solidified into ash lime
Like ammonite, will be sealed in a coffin

Billion years of chaos in bedrock
Enduring to be fossil plate's slide
Billion years later, an AI electron microscope
Will decipher inscription on the homo sapiens' fossil

Can also detect dreams of a fossilized Thalamus[1]?

[1] Inner part of the cerebrum, lying immediately anterior and ventral to the midbrain, the final relay station for the major sensory systems projecting to the cerebral cortex.

나방의 꿈

숲의 그늘 속에서
무채색의 날개를 나무 등걸에 펴고
낙엽처럼 엎드려서
들녘을 바라본다

눈 부신 햇살 속
꽃잎 위의 나비처럼
축문 가득한 날개를 세우고 싶어라

해 질 녘 밀실의 꽃술 속에서
향기 가득한 기억을 품고 싶어라

달빛이 스며드는 숲의 사잇길
가보지 못한 이적의 길인 듯
몽유의 유령처럼 무작정 날아본다

그늘의 덫을 지키는 거미에게
이생의 허물을 남겨주고
환생의 꿈을 품고
밤새워 날아본다

새벽 산책길에서 보는
지난밤 나방의 행적
전생의 데자뷰인지 낯설지 않다.

A Moth's Dream

In shade of forest
Spreading colorless wings on tree stump
Lying down like fallen leaf
Looking at a field

In dazzling sunlight
Like butterfly on flower petal
Wish setting wings full of blessings

In pistil of closed room at sunset
Wish holding memory full of fragrance

Forest path moonlight's seeping in
Like mysterious road, unexplored
Like ghost in daydream, flying aimlessly

To spider keeping trap of shade
Leaving exuviae of this life
Holding the dream of reincarnation
Flying all night long

On dawn walk,
Traces of last night's moth,
Not unfamiliar, as if deja vu from past life

메멘토 모리[1]

손목 시계의 초침이 돌아갈 때
핸폰 시계의 숫자가 바뀔 때
메멘토 모리
거실의 앵무새가 아침인사로 속삭인다

철 따라 꽃이 피었다 지는
출근길 아파트 담장 위에서
메멘토 모리
시든 꽃잎들이 바람에 속삭인다

손톱을 깎을 때처럼
텔로미어[2]의 꼬리가 잘려나가는 소리를
메멘토 모리
손목의 박동이 알려준다

라일락 밤 향기에 취해
퇴근길 하루살이처럼
끈끈이주걱 속으로 빨려 들어갈 때
메멘토 모리
경비원 아저씨가 내 손을 잡아주며 속삭인다

잠자리에서
살아온 가면을 벗고

Memento Mori[1)]

When second hand of wristwatch turns
When numbers on cell phone watch change
Memento Mori
A parrot in living room whispers good morning

Flowers' blooming and fading with seasons
On apartment fence on way to work
Memento Mori
Withering petals whisper in wind

Like cutting fingernails
Sound of telomeres'[2)] tail severing
Memento Mori
Pulse of wrist telling

Intoxicated by scent of lilac night
Like mayfly on way home
When get sucked into sundew
Memento Mori
Watchman holding my hand, whispering

In bed
Taking off mask lived in

죽어갈 거죽을 입을 때
메멘토 모리
나 자신에게 속삭인다.

1) "자신의 죽음을 기억하라"를 뜻하는 라틴어 말.
2) 세포 속에 있는 염색체의 양쪽 끝단에 있는 부분으로서, DNA를 보호하는 역할을 한다. 텔로미어는 세포의 노화와 밀접한 연관이 있다. 세포분열을 지속할수록 텔로미어가 줄어들어 염색체가 짧아지기 때문이다.

When wearing dying skin
Memento Mori
Whisperin to myself.

> 1) Memento mori, a Latin phrase meaning "remember your own death".
> 2) The ends of chromosomes in a cell that protect DNA and are closely linked to cellular aging. As cells continue to divide, telomeres shrink, resulting in shorter chromosomes.

잠들기

무덤 속에 누워 흙을 덮어쓰듯
이불을 뒤집어쓰는 잠버릇이 있다

어릴 적 우물 속으로 머리를 밀어 넣고
아, 하고 입안 가득히 고이는
초유의 모음을 뱉어서
아득한 울림을 볼살에 느껴본다

도망가다 지친 타조가 다리를 뻗고 엎드려서
흙 속에 머리를 파묻고, 죽음을 잠으로 맞이하듯이
가슴통 속으로 머리를 밀어 넣는다

어둠의 바닥에 모로 놓인, 깨어질 듯
들썩거리는 금박의 알을 본다

끝없는 목마름의 두레박질에 흔들리다
흉곽의 갈비뼈에 부딪혀 상채기가 생긴 것인가?
슬리핑 백처럼 이불을 뒤집어 쓰고도 잠들지 못하는 것이
알의 이마를 찌르는 가시 면류관 탓인가?

그래, 단단한 껍질의 타조 알처럼
그래, 터지지 않는 생고무 공처럼

Falling asleep

Like lying in grave, covering with earth
Have sleeping habit of pulling blanket over

Pushing head into a well in childhood
"Ah"
Spiting out vowel of first milk fulled in mouth
Sensing distant echoes in cheeks

An ostrich tired of running away, stretching out legs, lying down
Burying head in dirt, like welcoming death as sleep
Pushing head into chest

Lying with edge on the floor of darkness, as if might break,
Seeing gilded egg agitating

While shaking in endless thirst's bucket—drawing
Because of bruise struck by ribs of thorax?
Not falling asleep even pulling over blanket like sleeping bag
Because of crown of thorns piercing egg's brow?

Yes, like hard—shelled ostrich egg.
Yes, like rubber ball without popping.

원래 날지 못하는 날개이거니
원래 멍이 잘 드는 가슴이거니

아, 하고 목줄에 닻처럼 박힌
밤의 뼈다귀 한 소절을 뱉어놓고
부드러운 머드 팩의 베개 속으로
아늑한 무통의 질식 속으로
깊숙이 깊숙이 머리를 밀어 넣는다.

Because of wings without flight
Because of bruise-prone breast

"Ah", lodged like anchor on leash
Spit out a line of night's bone
Into a pillow of soft mud pack
Into cozy painless choke
Pushing Head into deep deep.

시계탑 06

휴대폰의 알람이 울린다

동녘의 해를 바라보며
백만 년을 걸어온 직립인의 심장에
태백의 정기를 주입하는 시각

잠 덜 깬 무릎관절을 펴고
웅크린 등뼈를 펴는 시각

하루의 만보를 시작하는 시각

가래 낀 목청을 틔우는 소리로
나뭇가지 둥지 속
까치들을 깨우는 시각

새로운 하루의 업을 여는 나에게
시계탑 위의 저승사자가
아파트 경비원 아저씨처럼 인사한다

이생의 남은 시간을 알려준다
어제의 이 시각보다
텔로미어[1]의 예상 잔존 시간이

Clock Tower 06

Cellphone alarm going off

Looking at rising sun
Into heart of upright man having walked million years
The time injecting Taebaek[1]'s energy

Stretching half−awake knee joints
The time straightening hunched spine

The time starting pace counter of today

With sound of clearing phlegm in throat
In nest of branches
The time waking magpies

To me opening karma of a new day
Grim reaper on clock tower
Greeting me like an apartment security guard

Telling time left for this life
Compared to this time yesterday
Estimated lifespan of telomeres[2]

4시간이나 더 많이 줄었다고

오늘은 가슴 가득
샛바람을 마시며, 풍선처럼
가볍게, 자유롭게
멀리 산과 하늘을 바라보며
노닐며 걷자.

1) telomere: 염색체의 말단에 존재하는 반복적인 염기서열을 가지는 DNA
조각으로서, 염색체 말단의 손상 혹은 근접한 염색체와의 융합으로부터
보호하는 역할을 수행한다.

Decreased by 4 hours'

Today, full of heart
Drinking east wind, like balloon
Lightly, freely
As looking at mountains and sky in distance
Let's roaming walking.

> 1) Short for Taebaeksan. A mountain on the border of Bonghwa-gun, Gyeongsangbuk-do, South Korea, and Taebaek-si, Yeongwol-gun, Gangwon-do, 1,567 metres high. It is known as the 'sacred mountain' of the Taebaek mountain range. (Translator's note)
> 2) The ends of chromosomes in a cell that protect DNA and are closely linked to cellular aging. As cells continue to divide, telomeres shrink, resulting in shorter chromosomes.

붉은 연어의 노래

활화산의 심장에서 솟구쳐 올라
골짜기의 폭포로 뛰어내려
하구의 제방을 타고 넘으며
강이, 바다로 달려간다

대동맥궁 솟대에 벼락이 치는 날
강에 쏟아지는 마그마들이
피톨이 되어 강물을 뜨겁게 달군다

붉은피톨의 유황내음을 되짚으며
꼬리지느러미로 귀천하는 붉은 연어
혓바닥들이 물살에 댓잎처럼 떨린다

그 모음의 주술 소리를 들으며
정수리 천문에서 부화한 치어들이
어미의 붉은 살점을 뜯어먹는다

등지느러미가 돛처럼 부풀 때
강의 발 끝에서 힘차게 방생되어
은하와 합류하는 먼바다로 간다

추락한 별들이 불가사리가 되는 해저에서
죽은 별들의 모음을 캐내면서,

Song of Red Salmon

Rising up from heart of active volcano
Plunging down into waterfalls of valley
Riding over banks of estuary
River, rushing to the sea

The day lightning strikes at spire of aortic arch
Magma pouring into river
Turning into blood cells, heating river

Remembering sulfurous smell of red blood cells
Red salmon returning to heaven with tailfins
Tongues quivering like bamboo leaves in currents

Listening to sorcery sound of the vowel
Fry hatched from parietal fontanel
Tearing, eating mother's red flesh

Dorsals fin swelling like sail
Releasing powerfully from river's toes
Going to distant oceans joining galaxy

On ocean floor of fallen stars turning into starfish
Diging up vowels of dead stars,

어미가 부르던 주술 소리를 듣는다
어부가 부르는 조상의 노래,
그 노랫말에서 강의 전설을 듣는다

수평선을 점화한 저녁 해의 홍염,
등지느러미에 성화로 채화하여
밤에도 빛나는 붉은피톨의 강,
그 시원의 분화구로 되짚어 간다

피톨의 유황냄새가 짙어질수록
연어의 몸비늘이 점점 붉어진다
강의 체온이 점점 뜨거워진다.

Hearing magic sounds sung by mother
Ancestral song sung by fisher,
In the words, hearing legend of river

Red flames of evening sun igniting horizon,
Putting torch on dorsal fin
River of red blood cells shining even at night,
Retracing to crater of the origin

As sulfur smell of blood cells stronger,
Salmon's scales turning redder and redder
Temperature of river growing hotter and hotter.

외치[1]의 꿈

5300년 결빙의 잠

조상의 오랜 믿음 대로
썩지 않는 육신과 소멸하지 않는 혼령,
그 증거물을 보여주고 싶었다
61가지의 문신을 새긴
멋진 몸틀을 보여주고 싶었다

몸 조각들이, 피톨들이
종자 씨앗이 되는
몸틀의 부활을 꿈꾸었다

질투의 돌화살에 박힌
왼쪽 어깨 상처의 통증을 견디며
인연의 끈을 잡고서, 부활을 꿈꾸며
핏자국을 남기며, 동면하는 곰처럼
빙하의 골짜기로 올라갔었다

설산에 별빛 총총히 박히는 밤에는
결빙의 속박에서 벗어난 혼령이
알프스 산장을 감싸고 내려온다

산기슭 아래,

Dream of Ötzi[1]

Frozen Sleep, 5300 Years

As ancestors' long belief
Incorruptible body and undying spirit,
Wished showing the proof
With 61 tattoos
Wished showing wonderful body form

Body fragments, blood cells
Becoming seed of species
Dreamed resurrection of new form

Pierced by stone arrow of jealousy
Enduring pain of wound on left shoulder
Holding on cords of karma, dreaming of resurrection
Leaving trails of blood, like hibernating bear
Climbing into valley of glacier

On snowy mountains, on starry night
Soul freed from frozen shackles
Descending upon, surrounding the Alps lodge

Below foothills,

볼차노 박물관[2] 냉동실 천장을
인광의 기파가 감싸고 있다

그런 날에는,
새 몸틀을 입고 와서
냉동실의 시린 유리 창문에 다가서는 사람,
따뜻한 피톨의 손바닥으로 어루만지며
빙판에 새겨진 외치의 증언을 되뇌는 사람

새롭게 환생한,
길거리에서 어깨 부딪히는
이웃 같은 그를 본다.

1) 이탈리아-오스트리아 국경 사이, 알프스 산맥의 외츠 계곡에서 발견된 약 5300년 전(청동기 초기) 중년 남성의 자연 냉동 미라.
2) 이탈리아 북부 볼차노에 있는 외치 아이스맨의 박물관.

Ceiling of the Bolzano Museum[2]'s freezer
Qi waves of phosphorescence surrounding

On such day,
Coming in new form
A Person approaching the freezer's cold glass window,
Caressing with palm of warm blood cells
Repeating testimony of Ötzi engraved in the ice

Newly reincarnated,
Bumping shoulder in a street
Seeing him like a neighbor.

> 1) A naturally frozen mummy of a middle-aged man, approximately 5300 years old (Early Bronze Age), found in the Ötz Valley in the Alps, on the Italian-Austrian border.
> 2) The Ötzi Iceman's museum in Bolzano, northern Italy.

‖ 해설 ‖

마리엘라 코르데로
시인 · 평론가 · 번역가

우주시론 시편들
절대에 도달하기 위한 여정의 탐구

김세영
시집

별빛의 화법

‖ Commentary ‖

BY Mariela Cordero
Poetry · critic · Translater

Cosmic Poetics Poetry
Seeking to Touch the Absolute

Say-young Kim
Poetry Collection

Narration of Starlight

우주시론 시
절대에 도달하기 위한 여정의 탐구

마리엘라 코르데로
(시인 · 평론가 · 번역가)

"시는 상징을 통해 절대에 다가가려는 시도이다". 스페인 시인 후안 라몬 히메네스(1881~1958)의 이 문구는 유사 이래 수많은 시인들의 탐구 정신을 드러냅니다. 히메네스에 따르면 시는 표현할 수 없는 것을 드러내고 상징과 은유를 통해 (미묘하게나마) 절대적인 것에 가닿으려 합니다. 그런 히메네스의 작품은 현실과 신비의 세계를 드나들며 진동합니다.

김세영 시인의 『별빛의 화법』 역시 헤아릴 수 없는 광활한 우주에 다가가 절대자에 도달하고자 하는 태고의 갈망을 드러낸 작품입니다. 그의 시에서 언급되는 과학의 개념들은 천체물리학적 현상에 대한 면밀한 고찰로 드러난 현실과 사실에 바탕하고 있습니다. 김세영의 시는 양자 물리학과 천체학을 실체적인 측면에서 탐구합니다.

무한한 우주의 비밀은 신비의 위대한 원천을 이룹니다. 김세영 시인은 과학과 영성을 연결합니다. 시인은 직접 자신의 작품에서 기와 리의 관계를 언급합니다. 리와 기는 하나로서가 아닌 상호 보완적 관계로 존재합니다. 리는 구조, 질

Cosmic Poetics Poetry
Seeking to Touch the Absolute

BY Mariela Cordero
(Poetry · critic · Translater)

《Poetry is an attempt to approach the absolute by means of symbols》. This phrase by the Spanish poet Juan Ramón Jiménez (1881−1958) reveals the quest of countless poets since the beginning of time. Poetry, according to Jiménez, seeks to express the ineffable and touch (even if subtly) the absolute through symbols and metaphors. His poetic work is at the epicenter of a tremor: between reality and mystery.

《Narration of Starlight》 by the poet Kim, Say−young is also on this ancient quest, reflecting this arcane, immemorial thirst for reaching the absolute, approaching the unfathomable vastness of the cosmos. It leans on reality and facts, as the scientific concepts mentioned in his poems reveal a careful investigation into astrophysical phenomena. Kim's poems explore quantum physics and astronomy from a very current perspective.

The infinite cosmos and its secrets represent a great source of mystery. The poet Kim also links science with spirituality. In the introduction the poet himself makes to his work, he references the relationship between Qi and

서, 자연법칙을 부여하며, 기는 우주를 드러내어 움직이는 역동적인 힘입니다. 기가 리에 따라 질서를 구현한다면, 리는 기가 질료적 사물에서 자연 현상의 전반에 이르기까지 형상적 형태로 조직화되어 나타나게 하는 방법론적 틀입니다.

과학과 영적인 것 사이의 융합은 그의 시 「새로운 약속(新約)」에서도 관찰할 수 있습니다:

>   성간을 건너가는 혜성처럼
>   입자의 틀을 빠져나온 파동처럼
>   주파수 공명을 찾아서 합류하며
>   장대한 기파의 강이 흐른다
>
>   궁수자리 A별[4]의 중심부를 뚫고
>   물질 우주의 웜홀[5]을 지나
>   화이트홀[6] 너머로
>   오로라처럼 솟구쳐 나가서
>   영성 우주로 건너갈 거야
>
>   우주새의 전언傳言처럼
>   새로운 약속의 예언대로
>   거대한 기파의 공명, 끝없는 성간 울림
>   영성의 법열로 거듭날 수 있을 거야.

입자 프레임, 웜홀, 혜성… 모든 것이 새로운 언약 속에서 춤을 추며 그 끝에는 법열이 있습니다. 그렇다면 어떻게 이런 특이한 융합이 일어날 수 있을까요?

우주의 신비와 심원함을 그려내는 시인은 이 시집을 구성하는 시편들을 우주시라고 부릅니다. 별, 행성들, 천문 현상의 탐구와 우주적 관조를 통해 철학적, 영적 질문을 탐색하는 김세영 시인의 시집은 그러한 시적 스타일의 전형을 제시하고

Li. Li and Qi complement each other and cannot exist without one another. Li provides the structure, order, and natural laws, while Qi is the dynamic force that animates and moves the universe. Qi needs Li to manifest in an orderly way. Li is the framework that guides how Qi is organized and manifests in tangible forms, from physical objects to natural phenomena.

This fusion between the scientific and the spiritual can be observed in the verses of his poem 《The New Covenant》:

> Like comet crossing interstellar
> Like waves escaping particle frame
> Finding, joining frequencies resonance
> The mighty Qi[4] waves river flowing
>
> Piercing through Sgr A*[5] heart
> Passing through material universe wormhole[6]
> Beyond white hole[7]
> Soaring forward like aurora
> Will going to cross into spiritual universe
>
> Like cosmic bird message
> As prophesied in new covenant
> Great Qi waves' resonance, endless interstellar echos
> Will be reborn in spiritual Dharma bliss.

Particle frames, wormholes, comets... Everything dances in a new covenant where at the end lies the bliss of Dharma. And how can this unusual confluence occur?

The poet Kim refers to the poetry that makes up this anthology as cosmic poetry. Exploring philosophical and spiritual questions through the exploration of stars, planets, astronomical phenomena, and cosmic contemplation, Say-

195

있습니다.

하나의 장르로서의 우주시는 이제 막 형성되기 시작했지만, 태고적부터 시인들이 영감과 그 해답을 찾기 위해 하늘을 바라보았다는 사실은 잘 알려져 있습니다. 수메르시는 기원전 3000년경 고대 메소포타미아에서 수메르인이 쓴 것으로 알려진 가장 오래된 문학 형식 중의 하나입니다. 점토판에서 발견된 일부 시의 유물에서는 하늘과 별, 자연 현상에 대한 수메르인들의 매혹을 반영하는 우주적 주제가 명확히 드러납니다. 달의 신「난나 찬가」는 달의 신의 위대함과 힘, 그리고 지구와 우주에 대한 신의 전능을 찬미합니다.

고대 그리스 시인 호머(기원전 8세기)의 작품에서 별은 항해 도구일 뿐만 아니라 운명과 우주적 질서의 심오한 상징이기도 합니다. 밤하늘의 별의 위치와 움직임은 신성한 법칙에 의해 지배되는 우주의 속성을 반영하며, 개인의 운명은 그들의 길을 안내하는 별들에 새겨집니다. 김세영 시인은 첫 시「소요유」에서 꿈을 암시합니다.

> 별들의 소리가 선명해지는
> 자정의 몽유처럼
> 꿈꾸며 노닐자
>
> 육신의 틀을 벗은 혼령처럼
> 입자의 틀을 벗은 파동처럼
> 시공의 틀을 벗은 양자처럼

자정의 몽유처럼/ 꿈꾸며 노닐자"는 삶이 물리적 현실의 제약 없이 꿈처럼 노닐며 탐험할 수 있는 환상일 수 있다는 생각을 불러일으킵니다. "시공의 틀을 벗은 양자처럼"은 양자 입자가 전통적 시공간의 제약을 벗어나 존재할 수 있다

young Kim's poetry collection presents the epitome of such poetic style.

While cosmic poetry as a genre is just beginning to take shape, it is well known that since time immemorial, poets have gazed at the sky in search of inspiration and answers. Sumerian poetry is one of the oldest known forms of literature, originating in ancient Mesopotamia by the Sumerians around 3000 BC. In the remains of some poems found on clay tablets, cosmic themes are evident, reflecting the Sumerians' fascination with the sky, the stars, and natural phenomena. The Hymn to Nanna, dedicated to the moon god Nanna (or Sin), celebrates the greatness and power of the moon god and his influence over the earth and cosmos.

In Ancient Greece, the poet Homer (8th century BC) in his works, the stars not only serve as navigation tools but also as profound symbols of destiny and cosmic order. The position of the stars and their movement through the night sky reflect the idea of a universe governed by divine laws, where the destiny of each individual is written in the very stars that guide their path. The poet Kim alludes to the dream in his first poem Roam Freely:

> Stars sound's growing clearer
> Like dream of midnight
> Let me play, dreaming
>
> Like spirit shedding body frame
> Like waves escaping particles pattern
> Like quanta transcending space−time form

≪Like dream of midnight / Let me play, dreaming≫ evokes the idea that life can be like a dream, an illusion in which the self can play and explore without the restrictions of physical reality. ≪Like quanta transcending space−time form≫ introduces a modern perspective where

는 현대적 관점을 소개하며, 생각보다 현실은 복잡하고 실체가 없다는 생각에 공감을 불러일으킵니다.

우주시라는 장르는 발전 중이지만 적어도 수세기 동안 우주적 조망이나 견해를 담은 시가 존재해 왔습니다. 그러한 시인 중 한 명은, 의심할 여지 없이, 화가이자 조각가이기도 했던 영국의 윌리엄 블레이크(1757-1827)로서 그는 풍부한 상상력과 환상적인 작품으로 주목을 끌었습니다. 블레이크는 그의 작품에서 우주적 창조력을 독특하고도 풍부한 상징의 형식으로 구현했습니다.

그의 작품에서 우주는 물리적 공간이며 영적 정신의 공간입니다. 그의 중심 개념의 하나는 물질계의 현실은 곧 영적 힘의 표현이라는 생각입니다. 블레이크에게 우주의 모든 것은 서로 연결되어 있으며 신성한 의도를 지니고 있습니다. 블레이크와 김세영 작품의 공유점을 간략히 조명해봅니다:

    타이거! 불타오르는
    밤의 숲,
    어느 불멸의 손과 눈이
    그대의 경외로운 대칭을 담아낼 수 있으랴?
                  - 윌리엄 블레이크,「타이거」부분.

    은하의 골짜기를 비추는
    기파氣波의 빛이여!
    영성靈性의 법열이여!
                  - 김세영,「오르가즘」부분.

블레이크는 한밤에 타오르는 호랑이의 눈빛을 통해 자연적 요소와 항성적 강렬함이 결합된 이미지를 보여줍니다. 어둠 속 호랑이의 이글거리는 빛은 광활한 우주의 천체와 공명합니다. 김세영 시인은 우주의 에너지를 직접적으로 표현

quantum particles can exist outside the traditional constraints of space−time, resonating with the idea that reality is more complex and less tangible than it seems.

As mentioned earlier, the genre of cosmic poetry is in development, but for centuries there has been at least poetry with a cosmic outlook or vision. One such poet is undoubtedly the Englishman William Blake (1757−1827), who was also a painter and engraver, and is recognized for his deeply imaginative and visionary work. In his work, Blake explored concepts of the universe and creation in a unique and richly symbolic way.

In his work, the universe is not just a physical place but also a spiritual and mental space. One of the central concepts in his work is the idea that material reality is an expression of spiritual forces. For Blake, everything in the universe is connected and has a divine purpose.

Briefly, I would like to illuminate the points of connection between a fragment of a poem by Blake and a poem by Kim:

>Tyger! burning bright
>In the forests of the night,
>What immortal hand or eye
>Could frame thy fearful symmetry?
>>William Blake (The Tyger)
>
>Light of Qi wave!
>Llluminating galactic valley
>Rapture of Spirituality!
>>Kim, Say−young (Orgasm)

Blake uses the image of the tiger ≪burning bright≫ in the ≪night≫, evoking a scene that combines natural elements with an almost sidereal intensity. The brightness of the tiger in the darkness resonates with the vision of a celestial object in the vast cosmos. The poet Kim uses the

하는 "은하의 골짜기를 비추는/ 기파氣波의 빛"이라는 이미지를 제시합니다. 두 이미지 모두 빛을 힘과 계시의 상징으로 사용합니다.

김세영 시인은 "기파의 빛"과 "영성의 법열"을 언급함으로써 우주를 비추고 형성하는 신적 또는 영적 에너지의 존재를 암시하며 우주 에너지와 창조 사이의 연관성을 강조합니다. 두 작품 모두 지상을 초월하는 이미지와 상징을 사용하여 우주시의 본질을 구현합니다.

우주적 비전을 가진 시인 그룹에 속하는 또 다른 시인은 의심할 여지 없이 독일 시인 프리드리히 횔덜린(1770-1843)입니다. 그의 작품은 자연, 영성, 우주의 깊은 연관성이 특징입니다. 그의 시는 종종 우주론적이며 신비로운 주제의 탐구를 통해 지각 가능한 것과 평범한 것 너머의 인식을 추구합니다.

무상함으로 사람들은 높은 곳을 오릅니다.
참으로 영묘한 빛을 향하여
– 횔덜린, 「신들이 걸었던 시절」 부분.

북극성에서 방출한 혼령의 빛이
...
악령을 제거하고 최적화시킨다
– 김세영, 「거듭나기」 부분.

두 시편에서 빛은 영적이고 미묘한 의미를 지닌 필수 요소로 사용됩니다. 횔덜린의 시에서 영적인 빛은 신실한 사람들이 지향하는 세계로서, 영적 승화와 신성한 도달을 의미합니다. 김세영의 시에서 북극성이 발하는 영적 빛은 악령을 제거하고 절대선을 이루며, 안녕과 구원의 힘으로 작용합니

image of the ≪Light of the Qi wave≫ that ≪illuminates the galactic valley≫, a direct representation of the cosmos and the energy that permeates the universe. Both images use light as a symbol of power and revelation.

The poet Kim, by mentioning the ≪Light of the Qi wave≫ and the ≪Rapture of Spirituality≫, suggests the existence of a divine or spiritual source of energy that illuminates and shapes the cosmos, emphasizing the connection between cosmic energy and creation. Both fragments embody the essence of cosmic poetry by using images and symbols that transcend the earthly.

Another poet who undoubtedly fits into this group of poets with a cosmic vision is the German poet Friedrich Hölderlin (1770−1843). His work is characterized by its deep connection with nature, spirituality, and the universe. His poetry often explores cosmogonic and mystical themes, seeking an understanding beyond the perceptible and the usual.

> With impermanent things: others climb higher
> To ethereal Light who've been faithful
>
> Hölderlin (Once Gods Walked)

> Spirit light emitted from North Star
> Removing and optimising evil spirit
>
> Kim, Say−young (Rebirth)

In both poetry fragments, light is presented as an essential element with spiritual and subtle connotations. In Hölderlin's poem, the ethereal light is reached by those who have been faithful, suggesting spiritual elevation and divine reward. In Kim's, the spiritual light emitted by the North Star has the power to remove and optimize evil spirits, acting as a protective and redemptive force.

다.

두시에서 빛은 상승과 순결의 형상을 상징합니다. 횔덜린의 시에서 미묘한 빛은 믿음과 인내를 통해 도달해야 할 목표이며, 김세영의 시에서 영적인 빛은 정화와 인도의 역할을 합니다. 두 텍스트에서 빛은 세속과 범상함을 초월하는 수단으로 작용합니다.

미국의 시인 월터 휘트먼(1819-1892)은 인간과 자연의 조화와 모든 생명체 상호 연결의 경이로움에 바탕하여 작품을 썼습니다. 휘트먼은 그의 시집 『풀잎』에 수록된 상징적인 시 「나의 노래」에서 개인과 집단의 정체성 그리고 자연과 우주를 찬미합니다.

> 나는 나를 축하하며 노래하고,
> 당신은 내가 생각하는 것을 생각할 것이니,
> 내 모든 원소는 당신의 것이기 때문입니다.
> — 월트 휘트먼(나의 노래)

월트 휘트먼의 시 「나의 노래」에서 "원소(atom)"라는 용어의 사용은 참신하고도 의미 있는 선택이었습니다. 과학적 용어를 시에 결합하는 것은 일반적이지 않았던 일로 휘트먼의 작품에서 "원소"의 언급은 혁신적인 시도였습니다. 서정시에 원자와 같은 과학적 개념을 사용하는 것은 과학적 지식과 시를 통합하는 방법이었습니다.

휘트먼이 그의 시에 과학적 개념을 도입한 것처럼 시인 김세영은 시 「거듭나기」에서 "양자"라는 단어를 사용합니다.

> 아득한 시공간 너머로부터

Light in both poems symbolizes a form of elevation and purity. In Hölderlin, the ethereal light is a goal to be achieved through faithfulness and perseverance, while in Kim, the spiritual light purifies and guides. In both texts, light acts as a means to transcend the earthly and the mundane.

Later in time, the American poet Walter Whitman (1819–1892) developed a poetic work based on the celebration of the unity of humanity and nature, and the interconnection of all living beings. In ≪Song of Myself≫: an emblematic poem from his collection Leaves of Grass, Whitman celebrates individual and collective identity, nature, and the cosmos.

> I CELEBRATE myself, and sing myself,
> And what I assume you shall assume,
> For every atom belonging to me as good belongs to you.
>
> Walt Whitman (Song of Myself)

The introduction of the term ≪atom≫ in Walt Whitman's poem ≪Song of Myself≫ was a novel and significant choice. Incorporating scientific terms into poetry was not common, making the mention of ≪atoms≫ in Whitman's work especially innovative. Including a scientific concept like the atom in a lyrical poem was a way to unite scientific knowledge and poetry.

In the poem ≪Rebirth≫, the poet Kim uses the word ≪quantum≫, just as Whitman included a scientific concept in his poem:

> Beyond faraway space−time

　　　　양자도약量子跳躍5)으로 다가온
　　　　새로운 생의 기파 마디들을
　　　　방전된 우주선을 공중 충전하듯
　　　　정수리 천문으로 주입시킨다

원자는 물질을 구성하는 반면, 양자는 에너지 상호 작용과 아원자 속성을 설명합니다. 휘트먼이 상호 연결성과 보편성을 상징하기 위해 그의 시에 원자의 개념을 도입하였듯이 김세영 시인은 오늘날 현대의 시 작품에서 "양자"를 사용하여 현대 과학 개념을 시적 영역에 통합하고 있습니다.

미국의 시인 윌리스 스티븐스(1879-1955)는 모든 존재의 통일성과 상호 연결성을 강조하는 휘트먼의 작품에 영향을 받아서 확장하였습니다.「가을의 오로라」는 스티븐스의 방대하고 복잡한 시로서, 총 10부로 구성되어 있습니다. 이 시에서 그는 변화와 무상이라는 주제를 탐구하기 위해 오로라를 중심 은유로 사용합니다.

　　　　이곳은 몸통 없는 뱀이 사는 곳.
　　　　그의 머리는 공기. 밤의 끝자락
　　　　하늘 아래 눈을 뜨고 우리를 주시합니다.

스티븐스는 '몸이 없는 뱀'의 이미지를 사용하여 편재하는 우주의 존재를 상징합니다. 뱀은 하늘과 땅, 알려진 것과 알려지지 않은 것 사이의 연속성과 연결을 상징합니다.

　　　　밤하늘,
　　　　은하의 나선 고리에 얽혀
　　　　상들이 도미노처럼
　　　　일어나고 쓰러진다
　　　　　　　　　　　　　　- 김세영,「얽힘」부분.

> Arrived through quantum jump[6)]
> Qi wave nodes of new life
> Like recharging a discharged spaceship in midair
> Injecting into a crown fontanelle

Atoms make up matter, while quanta explain energy interactions and subatomic properties. Whitman innovated by incorporating the concept of the atom in his poetry to symbolize interconnectedness and universality. Similarly, the use of ≪quantum≫ in modern poetry, as in Kim's work, incorporates contemporary scientific concepts into the poetic realm.

The American poet Wallace Stevens (1879−1955) was influenced by Whitman's work, which emphasizes the unity and interconnectedness of all beings. Stevens adopts and expands this approach, employing such images to explore reality and aesthetic experience, as in ≪The Auroras of Autumn≫. ≪The Auroras of Autumn≫ is an extensive and complex poem by Wallace Stevens, composed of ten parts. In it, Stevens uses the auroras boreales as a central metaphor to explore themes of change and impermanence.

> This is where the serpent lives, the bodiless.
> His head is air. Beneath his tip at night
> Eyes open and fix on us in every sky.

Stevens uses the image of the ≪bodiless serpent≫ to symbolize an omnipresent cosmic presence. The serpent represents continuity and the connection between heaven and earth, the known and the unknown.

> Night sky,
> Entangled in spiral ring of galaxy
> Statues, like domino
> Rising, falling
>
> Kim, Say−young (Entanglement)

"은하의 나선 고리에 얽혀"라는 구절에서는 복잡한 이미지가 제시됩니다. 나선 은하는 광범하고 장엄한 구조로서, 그 안에 얽혀 있다는 아이디어는 우주 만물의 복잡성과 상호 관계를 반영합니다.

도미노 같은 상들'은 흥미로운 시각적 은유를 제공합니다. 동상은 정적인 형상이지만 도미노에 비유하여 움직임과 변화를 나타냅니다. 이 은유는 움직이지 않는 것처럼 보이는 것조차도 역동적인 힘의 지배를 받는다는 것을 암시합니다.

스티븐스와 김세영은 두 시에서 밤하늘의 이미지를 사용하여 무한함과 신비감을 전합니다. 스티븐스는 밤하늘을 아우르는 형상인 "뱀이 사는 곳"을 언급하고, 김세영은 '별이 빛나는 밤'을 묘사합니다. 스티븐스의 북극광 "오로라 보레알"과 김 작가의 나선형 은하수는 우주의 심원함을 보여줍니다.

라틴 아메리카 시에는 비센테 후이도브로, 호르헤 루이스 보르헤스, 옥타비오 파스, 에르네스토 카르데날, 에우헤니오 몬테호, 세자르 발레호 등 우주적 시각을 지닌 시인들이 있습니다. 라틴 아메리카 시는 원주민, 콜럼버스 이전, 아프리카, 유럽 문화의 요소가 결합된 풍부하고 다양한 문화 유산을 가지고 있습니다.

칠레의 시인 비센테 후이도브로(1893~1948)는 시인이 현실을 모방하기보다는 새롭고 독창적인 세계를 창조해야 한다는 생각을 장려한 창조주의 운동의 창시자 중 한 명입니다. 이러한 접근 방식을 통해 보편적이고 추상적인 주제를 탐구할 수 있었기 때문에 우주적 비전을 가진 시인으로 분류할 수 있습니다.

태양이 선택한 우리는

In the verse ≪Entangled in spiral ring of galaxy≫, an intricate image is suggested. Spiral galaxies are extensive and majestic structures, and the idea of being entangled in them reflects the complexity and interrelation of all things in the universe.

≪Statues, like domino≫ provides an intriguing visual metaphor. Statues are static figures, but comparing them to dominoes implies movement and change. This metaphor suggests that even the seemingly immobile is subject to the dynamic forces.

In both poems, Stevens and Kim use images of the night sky to convey a sense of infinity and enigma. Stevens mentions ≪the place where the serpent lives≫, a figure that encompasses the night sky, while Kim describes ≪the starry night≫. Stevens' auroras boreales and Kim's spiral galaxies capture the grandeur of the universe.

Latin American poetry also has poets with a cosmic vision, including Vicente Huidobro, Jorge Luis Borges, Octavio Paz, Ernesto Cardenal, Eugenio Montejo, Cesar Vallejo, among others. Latin American poetry has a rich and diverse cultural heritage that combines elements of indigenous, pre-Columbian, African, and European cultures.

The Chilean poet Vicente Huidobro (1893-1948) was one of the founders of the Creacionismo movement, which promoted the idea that the poet should create a new and original world, rather than imitate reality. This approach allowed him to explore universal and abstract themes, which is why he can also be categorized as a poet with a cosmic vision.

  We were the sun's chosen ones
  And we didn't realize it

그것을 깨닫지 못했으며
가장 높은 별의 선택을 받은 우리는
은총에 어떻게 보답해야 할지 몰랐습니다.
　　- 비센테 후이도브로, 「우리는 태양의 선택받은 자」 부분.

동녘의 해를 바라보며
백만 년을 걸어온 직립인의 심장에
태백의 정기를 주입하는 시각
　　　　　　- 김세영, 「시계탑 06」 부분.

후이도브로의 시는 당시에는 고마움이나 이해가 없었던 우주의 선물에 대한 인식과 반응에 대한 성찰을 다루고 있습니다. "태양"과 "가장 높은 별"의 은유는 비록 완전한 이해는 없었지만 심원한 하늘과의 연결을 강조합니다.

김세영 시인의 시는 수백만 년을 여행해 온 호모 사피엔스로 의인화된 지구의 우주와 조상의 에너지에 대한 몰입을 다루고 있습니다. 그는 에너지의 연속성과 유산에 초점을 맞추어 우주와의 관계를 보다 완전하고도 강조적으로 표현합니다. '태양'은 두 시 모두에 등장하는 요소로 인간과 신 또는 우주를 연결하는 에너지, 생명, 힘의 원천을 상징합니다. 후이도브로는 응답의 부재를 반성하는 반면, 김세영 시인은 시간을 통한 지속적인 행동, 즉 그 항성 에너지를 흡수하고 전달하는 모습을 그립니다. 과거의 잃어버린 시간을 반성하는 후이도브로와 시간의 연속적 흐름 속에서 바라보는 김세영의 두 작품 모두 인간과 신의 이중성을 강조합니다.

작품에 우주적 비전을 표현한 시인들이 많아 일일이 언급하기에는 끝이 없지만, 각 시인들마다 독특하고 매혹적인 관점을 제시합니다. 하지만 라틴 아메리카에서 시와 우주적 비전을 융합한 또 다른 주목할 만한 인물은 니카라과의 에

> We were the chosen of the highest star
> And we did not know how to respond to its gift
> 			Vicente Huidobro (We were the sun's chosen one)

> Looking at rising sun
> Into heart of upright man having walked million years
> The time injecting Taebaek1)'s energy
> 			Kim, Say-young (Clock Tower 06)

Huidobro's lines address a reflection on the recognition and response to a cosmic gift that was not understood or appreciated at the time. The choice of the ≪sun≫ and the ≪highest star≫ as metaphors underscores a connection with the celestial and the grand, albeit without full understanding.

Kim's verses address immersion in the cosmic and ancestral energy of the earth personified by Homo sapiens who have traveled over millions of years. The poet Kim focuses on the continuity and heritage of the energy, emphasizing a more complete and expressed relationship with the universe. The use of the ≪sun≫ is an element present in both poems, representing a source of energy, life, and power that connects the human with the divine or cosmic. While Huidobro reflects on the lack of response, Kim shows a continued action through time, an absorption and channelling of that sidereal energy. Huidobro looks to the past, towards the missed opportunity, while Kim sees time as a continuous flow. Both fragments underline the duality of the human and the divine.

Since there are many poets who have expressed a cosmic vision in their works, it would be endless to mention them one by one, although each one offers a unique and fascinating perspective. However, in Latin America,

르네스토 카르데날(1925~2020)입니다.
(카르데날이 2020년에 사망하여 동시대성이 있기 때문에) 에르네스토 카르데날의 작품은 김세영의 작품과 보다 직접적이고도 가까운 작품일 것입니다. 두 시인 모두 과학과 양자 물리학적 인식과 발견에 깊은 열정을 드러내고 있습니다. 두 시인 모두 과학적 용어를 사용하여 단순한 문학적 차원을 넘어 우주적, 철학적 성찰의 영역에 봉헌된 방식으로 시를 전개합니다.

그의 작품 '우주 찬가'에서 카데날은 빅뱅, 행성, 양자, 천체물리학 현상과 같은 주제를 탐구합니다. 그의 시는 단순히 우주적 사건에 대한 내레이션이 아니라 깊은 경외심으로 우주를 노래합니다. 카데날의 작품은 과학적 접근 방식을 통해 시를 풍성하게 하고, 독자로 하여금 자신과 주변의 모든 존재에 대해 성찰하도록 초대합니다,

아직 해독되지 않은 것들을 포함하여. 마찬가지로 김세영 시인은 과학과 양자 개념을 활용합니다. 그의 작품은 원초적 에너지에 대한 깊은 매혹을 반영하여 초월성이 풍부한 시적 서사를 만들어냅니다. 시인 김세영은 이러한 용어를 영적이고 실존적인 주제를 탐구하는 도구로 사용하여 유형과 무형의 우주를 모두 아우르는 의미의 그물을 엮어냅니다.

김세영의 『별빛의 화법』은 특정 장르로서의 우주시의 토대를 마련하고자 하는 문학과 시의 역사에서 중요한 이정표라고 굳게 믿습니다. 김세영 시인의 작품은 이러한 시의 스타일에서 피할 수 없는 전범으로 자리매김되고 있으며, 시문학 분야에서 참신성과 독창성을 찾는 모든 이들이 즐겨 읽을 수 있을 것이라고 단언합니다.

역사의 여러 단계에서 수많은 시인들이 영감적 이유를 찾거나 헤아릴 수 없는 우주의 속성이 불러일으키는 수많은

another notable figure who has managed to fuse poetry with a cosmic vision is the Nicaraguan poet Ernesto Cardenal (1925-2020).

I believe the work of Ernesto Cardenal (perhaps due to his contemporaneity, since Cardenal died in 2020) is the one that can have a more direct approximation to the work of Kim, Say-young. In both poets, a deep passion for science, quantum physics, and its discoveries is revealed. Both use scientific terms to develop their poetry in a way that transcends the merely literary and is consecrated within the realm of cosmic and philosophical reflection.

In his work ≪Cosmic Canticle≫, Cardenal explores themes such as the Big Bang, planets, quanta, and astrophysical phenomena. His poetry is not just a narration of cosmic events but a celebration of them, presenting them with reverent awe. Cardenal's work has a scientific approach that enriches his poetry, inviting the reader to reflect on their existence and the existence of everything around them, including what they have not yet deciphered. Similarly,

Kim, Say-young also employs scientific and quantum concepts in his poetry. His work reflects a deep fascination with primordial energies, creating a poetic narrative rich in transcendence. The poet Kim uses these terms as a tool to explore spiritual and existential themes, weaving a web of meaning that encompasses both the tangible and the intangibly cosmic.

I firmly believe that the poetry anthology ≪Narration of Starlight≫ by the poet Kim, Say-young represents a significant milestone in the history of literature and poetry as it intends to lay the foundations of cosmic poetry as a particular genre. I can assert that Kim's work positions itself as an unavoidable reference in this style of poetry and its reading will be enjoyed by all those seekers of the novel and original in the literary field.

As previously mentioned, at different stages of history, numerous poets have lifted their gaze to the sky, to the

질문에 대한 답을 찾기 위해 무한한 밤하늘을 향해 시선을 들어 올렸습니다. 우주적 시선 또는 비전을 가진 시인들은 역사적 시대의 관점에서 우주에 자신만의 용어와 언어로 이름을 붙였으며, 우주에 대한 인간 지식의 진화를 점차적으로 반영해나갔습니다.

김세영의 작품은 이러한 맥락의 다각적인 접근 방식이 돋보입니다. 그의 시에는 양자 물리학, 새로운 이론, 우주의 비밀에 대한 새로운 개념과 깊은 연구가 드러나 있습니다. 김세영 시인의 이 독특한 관점은 단순히 희열과 열정을 드러내는 것이 아니라, 탄탄한 지식의 뒷받침과 정교한 방식으로 이러한 분출을 전달하는 방법을 보여주고 있습니다. 『별빛의 화법』에서 과학과 시적 예술의 결합은 김세영 시인이 첨단 과학 개념과 깊은 서정적 표현의 통합으로 새로운 표현 형식의 선구자가 되게 했습니다.

김세영 작가가 이 시집을 제작하는 데 쏟은 열정과 헌신은 놀랍습니다. 그는 일관된 과학적 이해를 바탕으로 한 방법론에 의존하고 있으며 이는 감탄할 만한 가치가 있습니다. 김세영은 과학적 용어를 단순한 문학적 장식으로 사용하는 데 그치지 않고, 이러한 개념을 사용하여 존재와 우주의 깊이를 탐구하고 표현함으로써 지적으로나 영적으로 공명하는 형식을 취하고 있습니다.

김세영의 작품은 그러한 목적을 달성하고 초월하는 기준이 된다고 결론을 내릴 수 있습니다. 우주적 렌즈를 통해 보편적인 주제를 다루고 통합하는 그의 능력은 미래의 시인들에게 높은 기준을 제시합니다. 그의 시 형식은 분명 다른 이들로 하여금 명백한 것을 넘어 과학적 지식과 예술적 창의성 사이의 연관성을 탐구하도록 영감을 줄 것입니다.▲

infinite or nocturnal azure in search of reasons for inspiration or in search of answers to the thousands of questions that arise before the unfathomable nature of the universe. These poets, with their cosmic gaze or vision, have named the universe from the perspective of their historical time, in their own terms and words, gradually reflecting the evolution of human knowledge about the cosmos.

Kim, Say-young's work stands out in this context for its versatile approach. In his poetry, an exhaustive investigation into quantum physics, new theories, and emerging concepts about the secrets of the universe is revealed. This peculiar perspective is not just a display of euphoria and enthusiasm, but the poet has known how to channel this effusion in a sophisticated manner, backing it up with solid knowledge. The combination of science and poetic art in ≪Narration of Starlight≫ makes Kim a precursor of new forms of expression, by integrating advanced scientific concepts with a deep lyrical expression.

The passion and dedication with which Kim, Say-young has crafted this anthology is remarkable. He has relied on a method based on consistent scientific understanding, and this is worthy of admiration. Kim is not content with using scientific terms as mere literary adornments; instead, he uses these concepts to delve into and express the depths of existence and the cosmos in a way that resonates both intellectually and spiritually.

I can conclude that Kim, Say-young's work achieves its purpose and becomes a transcendental reference. His ability to address and merge universal themes through a cosmic lens sets a high standard for future poets. His style will surely inspire others to look beyond the obvious and explore the connections between scientific knowledge and artistic creativity.

베네수엘라의 마리엘라 코르데로(1985)는 작가, 번역가, 시각 예술가, 변호사로 활동하고 있습니다. 제2회 이베로아메리카 시 콘테스트 에콰도르 오일러 그란다(2015) 1등, 스페인 단편시 콘테스트 트랜스팔라브르 @RTE 2015 III 1등, 스페인 국제시 콘테스트 #Aniversario PoetasHispanos 1등(2016) 등 여러 국제 시상을 수상했으며 프린스턴 페스티벌, Parque Chas 국제시 페스티벌 등 여러 국제 문학 콘퍼런스 및 페스티벌에 참가했습니다. 현재 시 전문 잡지 포에마메(스페인)의 #베네수엘라 시와 #세계 시인 섹션을 관리하고 있으며, 시 전문 잡지 『상징학연구소』의 편집자문이자 시지프스(상징학연구소 시문학패 운영위원회(SIGPS) 전문위원으로 활동하고 있습니다. ◢

Mariela Cordero, Venezuela (1985) is a writer, translator, visual artist and lawyer. She has won several international poetry awards, including first prize in the 2nd Iberoamerican Poetry Contest Euler Granda, Ecuador (2015), first prize in the Spanish short poem contest TRANSPalabr @RTE 2015 III, first prize in the Spanish International Poetry Contest #Aniversario PoetasHispanos (2016), and has participated in several international literary conferences and festivals, such as the Princeton Festival and the Parque Chas International Poetry Festival. She currently manages the #Venezuelan Poetry and #World Poets sections of the poetry magazine Poémame (Spain) and is an editorial advisor and member of the SIGPS (Symbology Institute Poetry-ilterature Plaque Steering Committee) of the *Symbology Institute*, a magazine specializing in poetry.◢

나의 우주시론

김세영
(시인 · 평론가)

최근 십여 년 전부터 새로운 장르인 우주시에 관심을 갖고 작품을 써오고 있다. 오늘날은 글로벌 시대를 넘어서, 달 표면에 인간의 족적이 찍히고, 우주여행의 베이스캠프인 우주선에서 장기간 기거하는 시대이다. 더 나아가 화성에까지 우주선이 착륙하고, 태양계 외곽 너머로 우주선이 성간 비행하는 우주시대가 되었다. 우주와 은하가 인간의 생활환경과 자연환경이 된 시대에 살고 있으므로, 우주적 소재에 대해서 그리고 우주적 인식을 가지고 시를 써보고 싶었기 때문이다.

My Cosmic Poetics

BY Kim, Say-young
(Poetry · critic)

In the last decade or so, I have been interested in and writing a new genre of the cosmic poetry. Today, we are beyond the global era, with human footprints on the surface of the moon and long-term residence on spacecrafta as a base camp for space travel. Furthermore, it has become a space age where spacecraft have landed on Mars and spacecrafts are flying interstellarly beyond the outer reaches of the solar system. Since we live in an era where space and galaxies have become our living and natural environments, I wanted to write poems with cosmic materials and cosmic awareness.

우주론: 현대 천체물리학적, 기철학적

우주에 관한 책들을 보면서 현대 천체물리학적 우주이론과 동양의 기철학적 우주론이 서로 근본적 개념이 일치한다는 점에 새삼 놀라움을 느끼게 되었다. 우주를 한마디로 표현한다면 공간과 시간의 총체라고 말할 수 있다. 우주에는 약 1000억 개의 은하가 존재하며, 태양계가 있는 '우리은하'는 그 가장자리에 위치하고 있다. '우리은하'에는 약 2000억 개의 항성이 있고, 그중에서도 태양과 같은 별은 약 1000억 개가 된다고 한다.

우주 생성의 가장 유력한 이론인 빅뱅우주론에 의하면, 약 138억 년 전 초고온, 초고밀도의 한 점에서 빅뱅이 일어나 우주가 탄생하였으며, 지금까지 계속해서 팽창하고 있다. 우주 생성의 시작점은 밀도가 무한대이고 부피가 0인 영역이며, 이것을 특이점(singularity)이라고 한다. 이 시간도 공간도 없는 상태에서 반지름이 $10-33cm$인 초극미 우주(우주알)가 탄생하였다고 한다.

이 시작에서부터 초팽창(인플레이션)이 일어났다. 이어서 대폭발(big bang)이 일어난 후 현재까지 우주가 계속 팽창 중에 있다고 본다. 우주가 팽창하여 온도가 낮아지면서 점차 무거운 입자가 생성되었다고 한다. 우주 초기에 수소와 헬륨이 생성되고 이들 원소를 재료로 해서 수억 년(4억~7억 년) 후 은하와 별이 탄생하였다.

원자 생성 이전의 우주는 전자가 우주 공간을 자유롭게 떠돌아다니었다. 빛과 전자가 충돌하여 빛이 직진하지 못해서 우주는 불투명하였다. 빅뱅 후 약 38만 년이 지나서, 우주의 온도가 3000K로 낮아졌을 때, 원자가 생성

Cosmology:
Modern Astrophysical and Qi-Metaphysical

As I read books about the universe, I was struck by how modern astrophysical cosmology and Eastern Qi-philosophical cosmology agree on fundamental concepts. If I had to describe the universe in one word, I would say that it is the totality of space and time. There are about 100 billion galaxies in the universe, and the Milky Way galaxy with our solar system is located at the edge of it. There are about 200 billion stars in the Milky Way, and about 100 billion of them are stars like the sun.

According to the Big Bang cosmology, the leading theory of the creation of the universe, the universe was born about 13.8 billion years ago at a point of ultra-high temperature and ultra-high density, and has been expanding ever since. The starting point of the universe's creation is a region of infinite density and zero volume, called a singularity. In this state of no time and no space, an ultra-fine universe (cosmic egg) with a radius of 10-33 centimeters was born.

From this beginning, super-expansion (inflation) occurred, followed by the big bang, and the universe is believed to have been expanding ever since. As the universe expanded, its temperature decreased, gradually creating heavier particles. In the early universe, hydrogen and helium were created, and galaxies and stars were formed from these elements hundreds of millions of years later (400-700 million years).

Before the creation of atoms, electrons roamed freely in space. The universe was opaque because light and electrons collided and light could not travel straight. About 380,000 years after the Big Bang, when the temperature of the universe dropped to 3000 K, atoms were created,

되면서 빛이 직진할 수 있게 되고 우주가 비로소 투명해졌다.

기철학에서는, 우주가 생성되기 전, 기가 무한히 흩어져 있는 상태를 태허太虛라고 하였다. 서양철학에서 케이오스(chaos)라고 부르는 상태이다. 우주의 기저바탕 (background)이리고 할 수 있다. 기가 서서히 모여들어서 기가 응결된 상태, 아직 양과 음이 분화되지 않은 상태를 태극太極이라고 한다. 이것이 바로 우주생성의 본체(core)이다. 이 극한으로 응축된 상태인 우주알(cosmic egg)이 대폭발한 것이 빅뱅이다. 기가 팽창하면서. 일부 기가 응결되어 우주가 생성되었다고 본다. 이 상황을 서경덕은 원리기原理氣에서 양고음취陽鼓陰聚라고 표현하였다. 즉 북을 치듯이 쿵 소리를 내며 터져나가고, 한편으로는 다시 기가 모여 응결되어 만물(별)이 생성되었다는 표현이다. 이러한 팽창의 종국에는 다시 태허의 상태로 돌아갈 것이라고 보고 있다. 이처럼 태허와 태극의 순환이 바로 우주의 순환이다.

현대 물리학에 의하면, 모든 물질은 1억분의 1cm 크기의 원자의 조합으로 이루어지고 있다고 한다. 또 이 원자는 5조분의 1cm 정도의 극히 작은 입자로 구성되고 있는데, 이 작은 입자에는 전자, 양자, 중성자 3종류가 있으며, 소립자라고 부른다. 이외에도 양자와 중성자를 연결시키는 중간자, 중성자의 붕괴로 생겨나는 뉴트리노(중성미자) 등 새로운 소립자가 계속 확인되고 있으며, 그 수는 현재 약 300개가 넘는다고 한다.

1960년대에는 실험에서 관측되는 숫자가 점점 증가하는 원자 구성입자들을 설명하기 위해 학자들이 고심했다. 이론 물리학자들은 양성자와 중성자가 더 작은 물질의 단위로 이

allowing light to travel straight, and the universe became transparent.

In Qi-philosophy, the state of infinite scattering of Qi before the creation of the universe is called the taiheo 太虛. In Western philosophy, it is called chaos. It is called the back background of the universe. The state in which Qi is gradually gathered and condensed, and in which the positive and negative are not yet differentiated, is called the taiheo. This is the core of the creation of the universe. The Big Bang is the explosion of the cosmic egg, which was in this extremely condensed state. As the Qi expanded, some of those condensed and the universe was created. In this context, Seo Gyeong-deok expressed it through the concepts of 'Li' (principle) and 'Qi' (vital energy), describing it as 'the bright Qi explodes like a drumbeat, while the dark Qi gathers and condenses to form all things (stars).' This means that the bright Qi bursts forth to create the universe, and the dark Qi then gathers to form all phenomena. At the end of this expansion, it is believed to return to the state of the taiheo. This cycle of the taiheo and the taigeuk is the cycle of the universe.

According to modern physics, all matter is made up of a combination of atoms that are one hundred millionth of a centimeter in size. These atoms are also composed of extremely small particles, about 5 trillionths of a centimeter in size, called elementary particles, which include electrons, protons, and neutrons. In addition, new subatomic particles are constantly being identified, such as the neutrino, which connects a proton and a neutron, and the neutrino, which is created by the decay of a neutron, and the number of these subatomic particles is currently over 300.

In the 1960s, scientists struggled to explain the ever-increasing number of atomic constituent particles observed in experiments. Theoretical physicists began to

루어져 있을 가능성을 추론하게 되었다. 1961년 미국의 머리 겔 만(Murray Gell-Mann)과 이스라엘의 유발 네만(Yuval Neman)의 두 물리학자는 강력으로 결합한 입자들을 구조 성분별로 설명하는 입자 분류구조를 제안했다. 1964년 겔 만은 그러한 구조의 물리적 기초로 쿼크(quark) 개념을 도입했다. 쿼크들이 결합하여, 양성자와 중성자가 생기게 된다. 또 양성자와 중성자가 결합하여 중수소의 원자핵과 헬륨의 원자핵이 생기게 된다. 이 수소와 헬륨의 원자핵에 전자가 결합하여 원자가 생기게 된다

양성자와 중성자가 원자핵을 이루는 것과 같이 양성자와 중성자 그 자체는 쿼크로 이루어져 있다고 생각한다. 양성자와 중성자 외에 다른 중입자들도, 핵의 구성성분을 결합하는 힘인 강력에 의해서 상호작용하는 모든 입자처럼 쿼크로 설명한다. 이 쿼크를 궁극적인 기본입자로 추정하고 있다. 쿼크는 내부 구조가 없는, 즉 더 작은 그 무엇으로 분리될 수 없는 입자이다.

동양의 기철학에서는, 이 우주 만물의 궁극적 실체, 근원적 요소를 기氣라고 명명하고 핵심 개념(key word)으로 삼고 있다. 기는 물질의 궁극적인 최소 질량단위이면서 에너지 단위라는 개념을 내포하고 있다. 이 기氣가 현대 입자 물리학에서 말하는 쿼크(quark)에 해당한다고 본다.

모든 존재 현상은 기가 모이고 흩어지는 데 따라 생겨나고 사라진다고 본다. 또한 기의 운동 법칙성 내지 내재적 속성을 리理라고 부른다. 그래서 기는 입자적 속성뿐만 아니라 운동성 및 파동성을 가지고 있으므로 기파氣波라고 표현하는 것이 적합하다고 생각한다. 그래서 필자의 시에서도 기파라는 용어를 시어로 사용하고 있다. 기철학에서는 이 기氣가 양

speculate that protons and neutrons might be made up of smaller units of matter. In 1961, two physicists, Murray Gell-Mann of the United States and Yuval Neman of Israel, proposed a particle classification structure that described strongly bound particles by their structural components. In 1964, Gell-Mann introduced the concept of the quark as the physical basis for such a structure. Quarks combine to form protons and neutrons. And protons and neutrons combine to form the nuclei of deuterium and helium. These hydrogen and helium nuclei combine with electrons to form atoms.

Just as protons and neutrons make up the nucleus of an atom, protons and neutrons themselves are thought to be made up of quarks. Other heavy particles besides protons and neutrons are also described as quarks, as are all particles that interact with the strong force, the force that binds the constituents of the nucleus. These quarks are thought to be the ultimate fundamental particles. Quarks are particles with no internal structure, that is, they cannot be separated into anything smaller.

In the Eastern Qi-philosophy, the ultimate reality, the fundamental element of all things in the universe, is named the Qi and is the key word. The Qi is the ultimate smallest unit of mass and energy of matter. It is considered to be the equivalent of a quark in modern particle physics.

It is believed that all existing phenomena arise and disappear according to the gathering and dispersal of the Qi. In addition, the movement law or intrinsic property of the Qi is called the Li. Therefore, since the Qi has not only particle properties but also kinetic and wave properties, I think it is appropriate to express it as the Qi wave. That is why I use the term Qi wave in my poem. In Qi-philosophy, it is said that this Qi is divided into two types, one that has the properties of positive and the other that has the

陽의 성질을 가지고 있는 것과 음陰의 성질을 가진 것으로 분화된다고 한다. 이것은 현대 물리학에서 소립자를 양의 전하를 가지고 있는 것(양성자)과 음의 전하를 가지고 있는 것(전자)으로 나누는 것과 일치하는 것이 놀랍다.

우주시: 우주서정시와 우주영성시

현대물리학적 및 기철학적 우주론의 바탕개념 위에서, 우주적 시공간과 현 세계의 사물들을 융합적으로 느끼고 사유하는 것이 필요하다고 생각되었다. 이처럼 우주적 상상력으로 시세계를 확장해서, 최근 십여 년간 수십 편 이상의, 새로운 장르의 우주시들을 쓰고 발표해 왔다,

우주시란 어떤 시인가? 우주시를 한마디로 정의한다면, 우주에 대한 현대 천체물리학적 사실 인지와 이것을 바탕으로 한 세계 현실의 새로운 인식과 감성으로 쓰여진 시이다. 자연을 대상 소재로 하여 이에 대한 동일성의 인식과 감성의 바탕으로 쓴 시를 기존의 자연서정시이라고 한다면, 그 자연의 바탕을 우주적 시공간으로 확장 시킨 시가 우주시라고 정의할 수 있겠다. 우주의 중심이 지구라고 믿었던 시대에서의 자연서정시와, 칼 세이건에 의해서 처음으로 보여졌던 한낱 '창백한 푸른 점'에 지나지 않는 지구라는 행성에서의 자연서정시 즉 우주시는, 그 시적 바탕인 세계인식의 차원에서 엄청난 차이가 날 수밖에 없다.

1990년 2월 보이저 1호가 태양계의 외곽에서 카메라를 지구 쪽으로 돌려서 바라본 지구는 티끌 만 한 하나의 점에 지나지 않았다. 칼 세이건이『창백한 푸른 점』이란 그의 저서

properties of negative. It is surprising that this corresponds to the division of elementary particles in modern physics into those with a positive charge (protons) and those with a negative charge (electrons).

The Cosmic Poetry: the Cosmic Lyric Poetry and the Cosmic Spiritual Poetry

Based on the basic concepts of modern physical and Qi-philosophical cosmology, it was deemed necessary to feel and think about the convergence of cosmic space-time and things in the present world. In this way, by expanding the world of poetry with cosmic imagination, I have written and published more than dozens new genres of the cosmic poem over the past ten years.

What kind of poetry is the cosmic poetry? If I were to define the cosmic poetry in one word, it would be the poetry written with the new perception and sensibility of world reality based on the recognition of modern astrophysical facts about the universe. If the poem written based on the recognition and emotion of identification with nature as a subject matter is the conventional nature poem, the poem that expands the base of nature to cosmic space and time can be defined as the cosmic poem. There is a tremendous difference between the natural lyric poetry in the era when the center of the universe was believed to be the earth, and the natural lyric poetry, that is, the cosmic poetry, in which the earth as a planet is nothing more than a 'pale blue dot' first shown by Carl Sagan, in terms of the world perception underlying the poetry.

In February 1990, when Voyager 1 turned its camera toward Earth from the outer reaches of the solar system, the Earth was nothing more than a mere speck. I believe that the feeling and perception of that moment, described

에서 기술한, 그 당시의 감회(느낌과 인식)가 자연서정시로서의 우주시의 정서적 및 인식적 바탕이 된다고 생각한다.

오늘날의 현대시에는 양극단에 전통적 서정시와, 미래파적 실험시, 초현실적 시가 있다. 그 사이에 여러 경향의 시들이 산재해 있다. 그러나 아직도 여전히 현대시의 본령은 서정시라고 여겨진다. 그러므로 우주시에서도 우주적 소재와 소우주인 인간의 내면 정서를 결부시켜 은유적으로나 상징적으로 표현하는 자연서정시로서 자리매김을 할 수 있다고 본다. 이처럼 새롭게 확장된 장르로 발전시킨 시를 우주서정시라고 명명하면 좋겠다.

일론 머스크가 이끄는 민간우주기업 '스페이스X'가 화성우주선 '스타십'의 다섯 번째 시험 비행을 성공적으로 끝마쳤다고 시험 비행 성공을 알렸다.(2024.10.13. 보도) 워싱턴 포스트(WP)에 따르면 머스크는 앞으로 2년 안에 화성에 약 5개의 무인 스타십을 발사할 계획이라고 밝혔다. 무인 스타십이 화성에 안전하게 착륙한다면 앞으로 4년 안에 유인 임무도 수행할 가능성이 있다고 전한 바 있다. 조만간 우주가 인간의 실생활 공간 환경이 되는 시대가 도래할 것이라고 예상한다. 그때는 우주서정시가 특별하지도 않은 그냥 지금의 서정시가 될 것이다.

기철학에서 말하는 만물의 기본적인 단위인 기氣에 리理가 내재 되어 있듯이, 물질의 우주 세계에는 영성 우주세계가 내재 되어 있을 것이라고 상상해 본다. 현대 이론물리학자인 막스 플랑크(Max Planck)는 모든 물질은 어떤 힘에 기대어서만 발생하고 존재하며, 이런 힘의 바탕에는 의식적이고 지적인 마음이 분명 존재한다고 하였다.

by Carl Sagan in his book Pale Blue Dot, becomes the emotional and cognitive basis of the cosmic poetry as natural lyric poetry.

Today's contemporary poetry has the traditional lyric poetry, the futuristic experimental poetry, and the surrealist poetry at one end of the spectrum. In between, there are poems of different tendencies. However, the main spirit of modern poetry is still considered to be lyric poetry. Therefore, even in the cosmic poetry, it can be positioned as a nature lyric poem that connects cosmic materials with the inner feelings of humans, a microcosm and expresses them metaphorically and symbolically. This newly expanded genre of poetry could be named cosmic lyric poetry.

SpaceX, a private space company led by Elon Musk, has announced the successful completion of the fifth test flight of its Mars spacecraft Starship(October 13, 2024). According to the Washington Post, Musk plans to launch about five unmanned Starships to Mars in the next two years. It has been reported that if an unmanned Starship lands safely on Mars, there is a possibility that a manned mission will be carried out within the next four years. It is expected that the era in which space becomes a real-life space environment for humans will soon arrive. At that time, the cosmic lyric poetry will be nothing special, just the lyric poetry of today.

Just as the Li is inherent in the Qi, the fundamental unit of all things in Qi-philosophy, I imagine that the spiritual cosmic world is inherent in the material cosmic world. Max Planck, a modern theoretical physicist, said that all matter arises and exists only in dependence on some force, and that at the base of this force there must be a conscious and intelligent mind.

융(Jung, Carl Gustav)은 죽음이라는 것은 신체의 족쇄로부터 의식이 자유로워지는 것이라고 느꼈다. 윤회하는 영혼을 모나드라고 하며, 이 개념은 그리스 어원의 영혼의 기본단위 단자이다. 우주의 영성세계로 돌아가는 기본실체로 본다. 죽어서 육신이 분해되어 물질의 기본단위 소립자인 커크가 되어, 지구의 흙, 궁극적으로는 우주의 물질세계로 돌아가는 것과 같은 이치라고 생각한다.

대그리스의 피타고라스 학파 때부터 우주의 궁극적인 실체의 근원적인 기본단위로서 사용한 모나드(monad)는 비국소적 확률적 그리고 양자역학적 개념의 단위로도 원용되고 있다. 기철학에서 말하는 우주의 근원적 단위인 기와 동일한 개념의 기본요소라고 말할 수 있다. 이 양자 모나드가 영혼의 기본단위로 간주되고 있다. 비국소적 양자기억 정보의 전이(양자도약)를 통해서. 양자 모나드(영성 기억)을 시공간의 제약 없이 공유할 수 있다고 본다. 더 나아가 환생의 전이양태라고 상상적 추론을 할 수 있을 것이다.

이기파가, 이 에너지 파동의 힘이 즉 이 마음(理)이, 우주의 섭리라고 흔히 표현하는 우주의 현상에 내재하는 창의적인 원리이며, 우주의 정신, 우주의 혼이라고 부를 수 있을 것이다. 그리고 이 우주의 혼을 신의 속성이라고 할 수 있을 것이다. 이것은 범신론적이며, 스피노자(Spinoza)의 자연신(Deus sive Natura)과 같은 개념이다. 그러므로 우리의 모든 창의적 행위에서 우리는 그 속에 내재하는 신과 조우할 수 있다고 생각한다. 이러한 우주의 리, 영혼을 인식하고, 우주의 내밀한 순리의 이야기를 표현한 시가 바로 우주 영성시이다.

▲

Carl Gustav Jung felt that death was the liberation of consciousness from the shackles of the body. He called the reincarnating soul a monad, and this concept is the basic unit of the soul from Greek origin. I see it as the basic entity that returns to the spiritual world of the universe. I think it is the same principle as when we die, our physical body breaks down and becomes the basic particle of matter, quarks, which returns to the soil of the Earth and ultimately to the material world of the universe.

The monad, which has been used since the Pythagoreans in ancient Greece as a fundamental unit of ultimate reality in the universe, is also used as a unit of non−local stochastic and quantum mechanical concepts. It can be said to be the fundamental element of the same concept as the Qi, the fundamental unit of the universe in QI−philosophy. This quantum monad is considered to be the basic unit of the soul. Through the transfer of non−localized quantum memory information (quantum leap), the quantum monad (spiritual memory) can be shared without the limitations of space and time. Furthermore, it can be imaginatively inferred that it is a transitive form of reincarnation.

This Qi wave, the force of this energy wave, that is, the Mind (Li) is the creative principle inherent in the phenomena of the universe, which is commonly referred to as cosmic providence, and may be called the spirit of the universe, the soul of the universe. And we might call this cosmic soul the attribute of god. This is pantheistic, and is the same concept as Spinoza's Deus sive Natura. Therefore, in all of our creative endeavors, I believe we can encounter the god inherent in them. The poetry that recognizes this cosmic spirit or soul and expresses the story of the intimate order of the universe is exactly the cosmic spiritual poetry.

∥ 발문 ∥

『별빛의 화법』

우주와 고대의 순환이 일으키는 신명의 장력

정과리 (정명교)
(문학평론가 , 연세대학교 명예교수)

김세영 시의 특징은 시대와 공간을 폭넓게 아우르는 풍부한 지식을 바탕으로 자연과학의 새로운 발견과 고대로부터의 지혜를 깔끔하게 연결시키는 데서 돋보인다. 가령 첫 시, 「소요유」에서 시인은 뉴턴적 물리학을 벗어나는 양자 현상과 도가의 질곡 없는 자유 사이에 등호(等號)를 놓는 재치를 보여주는가 하면, 두 번째 시, 「새로운 약속」에서는 21세기 들어 특별히 부각된 우주 현상들의 강렬한 형상을 제시하면서 그것들에 대한 물음을 중세 기사도의 성배탐구에 비유함으로써 형상의 매혹과 진리에 대한 열정을 동시에 북돋는다.

이러한 시쓰기는 적어도 두 가지 미덕을 제공한다. 하나는 미래와 고대를 상충적으로 대립하는 것이 아니라 생명과 우주의 진화사를 통째로 관통하는 근본적 원리의 상통적 현상들로 이해함으로써, 그의 시가 인류의 지식을 증대시키는 장치로서 기능한다는 것이다. 즉 새롭게 나타난 신선한 앎과 오래 익어 신뢰를 주는 지혜를 순환적으로 이어줌으로써,

Afterword

Narration of Starlight

The Divine Tension of Cosmic and Ancient Cycles

Jeong, Gwa-ri (Jeon Gmyeong-gyo)
(Literary critic, Professor Emeritus, Yonsei University)

The characteristic of Kim Say-young's poetry stands out in that it neatly connects new discoveries in natural science with wisdom from ancient times based on a wealth of knowledge that broadly covers time and space. For example, in the first poem, "Roam Freely" the poet deftly draws an equal sign between the quantum phenomena that escape Newtonian physics and the unbounded freedom of the Taoist, while in the second poem, "The New Covenant," he presents powerful images of cosmic phenomena that have come to the forefront in the 21st century, and likens the questioning of them to the medieval chivalric quest for the Holy Grail, thereby simultaneously encouraging the fascination of form and the passion for truth.

Such poetry offers at least two virtues. By understanding the future and the ancient not as antagonistic opposites, but as homologous manifestations of fundamental principles that run through the evolutionary history of life and the

독자들로 하여금 버리는 지식이 없이 모든 앎들을 좀 더 열린 새로운 앎을 위한 질료들로 받아들이게끔 하는 것이다. 독자들은 그 질료들을 스스로 반죽하고 가공할 즐거움을 얻게 될 것이다.

다른 하나의 미덕은 시의 형상성이다. 가령 다음과 같은 시구를 보자.

>개망초 꽃잎이 발에 밟혀도
>매미가 솔방울처럼 발길에 차여도
>산책길에서는 자연스러운 일이다
>
>깨어있는 많은 날
>노심초사하며 심지를 다 태워 버리고
>안식의 집에 들어가는 것도
>자연스러운 퇴장이다
>
>세상에 갇혀 살았으니, 이제는
>벌거숭이 천문의 시냅스를
>당산나무 가지처럼
>언덕에 세우면 된다
>
>굽은 손가락 사이로
>마지막 남은 기파가 빠져나갈 때까지
>
>손바닥 속, 이승의 기억을
>벽조목 염주처럼 여물어지도록
>매만지고 다듬는 것이
>나의 마지막, 자연스러운 일이다.
>
>붕어빵 한 봉지의 뼛가루로
>산의 풀숲에 뿌려지는 것도
>자연스러운 마무리이다

universe, his poetry functions as a device for increasing human knowledge: by cycling between new, fresh knowledge and old, trusted wisdom, the reader is invited to accept all knowledge as materials for new, more open knowledge, without discarding any of it. Readers will have the pleasure of kneading and processing those ingredients themselves.

The other virtue is poetic formality. Consider, for example, a poem like this.

> While fleabane petals are tramped underfoot
> Cicada kicked by foot like pinecone
> Natural, walking the path
>
> Many waking days
> Burning all worried wicks
> Also entering house of rest
> Is natural exit
>
> Having lived trapped in world. now
> Naked fontanel synapse
> Like branches of dangsan-tree1)
> Let's set on hill
>
> Between bent fingers
> Until last remaining Qi wave has escaped
>
> In palm, memory of this life
> Until hardens like jujube prayer beads
> Polishing and refining
> My last, natural act.
>
> Like bone powder of a fish-shaped bread bag

>   보이저호가 헬리오포즈를 벗어나듯
>   우주여행을 떠나는 것은
>   자연스러운 버킷리스트이다
>
>   상여 노래를 애달피 부르지 마라
>   흑인 영가라도 흥겹게 부를 일이다
>   흰나비처럼 날개 펄럭이며
>   버선코 세우고 승무를 출 일이다.

「자연스러운 일」 전문이다. 일생을 마무리하는 노인의 마음이 차분히 부조되고 있다. 이렇게 자연스럽게 정리하는 자세는 드문 일은 아니고 아주 흔하게 표현되는 것 중의 하나이다. 시인은 그런 예사로운 마음을 그대로 취하되, 두 방향으로 연장시킨다. 한 방향은 오랫동안 인류에 평안의 지혜를 제공해 온 종교와 자연의 상징물들에게로 나아가는 것이다. 이는 운명을 넉넉히 받아들이는 긍정의 마음을 화자와 독자의 가슴 밑바닥에 뿌려주면서 주위의 온 세상에 다사로운 빛처럼 퍼져나간다. "흑인 영가"와 "승무"가 마지막에 등장하는 건 그런 분위기를 인상적으로 새기도록 한다.

그런데 이런 시쓰기는 많은 시인들이 자주 해 온 것이기도 하다. 김세영의 시는 바탕으로 주어진 마음 자세를 또 하나의 방향으로 이끌음으로써, 이 평안한 분위기에 이색적인 색감을 준다. 마지막에서 두 번째 연이 마지막 연에 이르는 분기기(分岐機)의 역할을 한다. "보이저호가 헬리오포즈를 벗어나듯"은 거의 반 세기전에 지구를 떠나 태양의 모든 혹성들을 관찰하며 그 정보를 송신하는 원대한 임무를 완수하고 이제는 태양계의 막바지를 관통하며 그 너머의 우주로 나아가고 있는 탐사선 보이저의 모습을 가리킨다. 이 모습을 통해서 안식의 여정은 문득 신생을 향한 새 출발의 형상으로 변신

> Also scattering in mountain grass
> Is natural ending
>
> Like Voyager leaving heliopause2)
> Space travelling
> Is a natural bucket list
>
> Don't sing death song with sorrow
> Sing even a black spiritual with joy
> Fluttering wings like white butterfly,
> Lift up socks toe, dance Buddhist dancing

It is the full text of 'Natural Things,' calmly depicting the mind of an old man ending his life. This natural way of organizing attitude is not uncommon, but one of the most common expressions. The poet takes the same sentiment and extends it in two directions. One direction is to the symbols of religion and nature that have long provided humanity with the wisdom of peace. This scatters a positive mind that generously accepts fate to the depths of the speaker and readers' hearts, and spreads like a warm light to the entire world around them. The final appearances of the "black chant" and "Buddhist dancing" serve to emphasize this mood.

However, this type of poetry writing is something that many poets have done frequently. The penultimate stanze acts as a turning point leading to the final stanze. "Like Voyager leaving heliopause" refers to the probe Voyager, which left Earth nearly half a century ago, fulfilling its grand mission of observing and transmitting information about all of the sun's moons, and is now traveling through the final reaches of the solar system and into space beyond. In this image, the journey of repose is suddenly transformed into a figure of renewal. Voyager has already exhausted its power reserves, but through a combination of self-

한다. 보이저는 이미 비축한 전력을 다 써버렸다. 그러나 자가 발전과 주변 에너지 흡수라는 방법을 통해 지구 조정실의 도움 없이 스스로 전력을 생산하며 저 너머로 끈기있게 나아가고 있다. 그 자발적 운동에 의해서 종말을 향해가는 도정은 신생으로 나아가는 도정으로 변화한다.

이 변화가 마지막 연에 결정적인 빛깔을 입힌다. '흑인영가'는 흥겨운 리듬을 타고 인종해방의 전진을 노래하는 느낌을 준다. 승무는 춤추는 사람이 버선코를 세우는 것과 동시에 날개를 달고 비상한다. 조지훈의 「승무」의 포인트는 고깔에 있었다.

　　　이밤사 귀또리도 지새는 三更인데
　　　얇은 紗 하이얀 고깔은 고이 접어서 나빌네라

옛 시인도 비상의 이미지를 고깔에 입힌다. 그러나 이 이미지는 꿈 속에 거주한다. "귀또리도 지새는 삼경"에 고깔은 "고이 접"히고 있다. 그래서 그 앞에 "복사꽃 고운 뺨에 아롱질 듯 두 방울이야 / 세사에 시달려도 번뇌는 별빛이라"는 구절이 나왔던 것이다. 반면 김세영 시인의 승무에서 독자의 눈길은 '버선코'에 쏠린다. 그 코에는 날아오르고자 하는 기운이 환하게 빛난다.

김세영 시의 우주와 고대의 순환은 선명한 형상을 입고서 독자를 일종의 신명 속에 돌입시킨다. 그 신명은 새로운 앎을 향한 호기심이기도 하며 동시에 스스로 과거의 중력을 탄력으로 삼아 미래를 향해 뻗쳐나가는 몸의 신명이기도 하다. 많은 독자들이 이 즐거운 은하철도에 동승하시기를 바란다.▲

generation and absorption of ambient energy, it generates its own power without the assistance of Earth's control center and perseveres beyond. Through that voluntary movement, the journey toward the end is transformed into a journey toward new life.

This change gives the final verse a decisive color. 'Black Spiritual' adds the feeling of singing about the advancement of racial liberation with a lively rhythm. The Buddhist dancing takes flight with wings at the same time as the dancer "Lift up socks toe". The point of Jihun Jho's "Seungmu" (Buddhist dancing) was "goggal" (butterfly-like hat).

> Even cricket sleepping, deep night.
> Thin white hood is a butterfly folded quietly
> — by Jihun Jho

The old poet also adds the image of wings in a hood (goggal), but this image resides in dreams. "Cricket sleepping, deep night" the hood (goggal) is "folded up." That's why there was a phrase before that, "drop drop on fair face of radiant flower / Even swaying in life, sorrow are starlights." In Say-yeong Kim's "Seungmu", on the other hand, the reader's eyes are drawn to the 'socks toe'. Its toe shines with the energy to soar.

The cosmic and ancient cycles of Kim's poetry take on vivid forms and plunge the reader into a kind of divinity. This is both the curiosity for new knowledge and, at the same time, the deity of the body that stretches toward the future using the gravity of the past as elasticity. I hope that many readers will join this enjoyable galactic railroad.

English Translation: Euisu Byeon (poet · critic)